Management for Professionals

More information about this series at http://www.springer.com/series/10101

Jan Y. Yang • Lei Chen • Zheng Tang

Chinese M&As in Germany

An Integration Oriented and Value Enhancing Story

Forewords by
Hermann Simon
Wang Weidong

Springer

Jan Y. Yang
Simon-Kucher & Partners
Strategy & Marketing Consultants
Cologne, Germany

Lei Chen
Shaangu Europa Forschung und
Entwicklung GmbH
Frankfurt am Main, Germany

Zheng Tang
China International Investment
Promotion Agency (Germany)
Frankfurt am Main, Germany

ISSN 2192-8096 ISSN 2192-810X (electronic)
Management for Professionals
ISBN 978-3-030-07598-9 ISBN 978-3-319-99405-5 (eBook)
https://doi.org/10.1007/978-3-319-99405-5

This Springer imprint is published by the registered company Springer Nature Switzerland AG
The registered company address is: Gewerbestrasse 11, 6330 Cham, Switzerland

Chris Yu and Wang Ziran of Simon-Kucher & Partners and Liang Shuanglin, Feng Yuxuan, and Zuo Wei of China International Investment Promotion Agency (Germany) also contributed to this study.

With the generous support of Simon-Kucher & Partners

SIMON • KUCHER & PARTNERS
Strategy & Marketing Consultants

Foreword by Prof. Dr. Dr. h.c. mult. Hermann Simon, Honorary Chairman of Simon-Kucher & Partners

If asked to name the most important economic trend of recent times, my unequivocal answer would be globalization. In 1900, global per capita exports amounted to six US dollars; by 2016, this number had reached 2081 dollars despite a world population five times larger than it was at the turn of the twentieth century. When China became the leading export nation in 2009, it was covered extensively by the media. We understandably focus much of our attention on exports but often overlook another key feature of globalization, namely that of international mergers and acquisitions (M&As) and foreign direct investment (FDI). German firms have been making significant investment in China since the year 2002, but serious cross-border M&A activities by Chinese companies in the other direction are a very recent phenomenon. It was only in 2016 that the value of Chinese FDI transactions in Germany surpassed the value of German FDI in China for the first time. China's leap to the top of the rankings has attracted considerable attention, but reactions by politicians, business leaders, the media, and the public have been mixed: will the Chinese overrun German businesses, or is the arrival of the Chinese helping German enterprises, particularly mid-sized companies, to succeed in China's vast market and compete more effectively in Globalia? Although information on this topic has been severely lacking, this book provides substantial answers to questions such as these. While it is too early to judge the long-term success of the most recent acquisitions, such as those of Kuka by Medea and KraussMaffei by China National Chemical Corporation, the three in-depth case studies presented here provide a well-grounded evaluation: Dürkopp Adler, a German hidden champion in industrial sewing machines, was acquired by SGSB in 2005; the Chinese buyer subsequently completed further acquisitions in the same sector. Joyson Electronics, a private enterprise, bought the automotive supplier Preh in 2011, before adding several other specialized suppliers to its portfolio. CIMC acquired Ziegler, an insolvent manufacturer of firefighting equipment, in 2013, allowing the company to expand into this new business area.

The case studies in this book are first rate. I would even go so far as to say that they are on a par with Harvard Business School cases. More importantly, they reveal spectacular successes. Both Dürkopp Adler and Ziegler were in deep trouble before they were acquired by investors from China but are now flourishing. In my opinion, there is no doubt that the Chinese owners have been more prudent in handling their newly adopted children than, for instance, American acquirers. They obviously understand the hidden potential of these German Mittelstand firms and haven't destroyed their company cultures. Although I have been observing these developments quite closely, I must admit that this book was eye-opening for me. I don't know whether the three cases are representative; however, I have heard similar comments regarding other cases, such as Putzmeister, which was acquired by Sany in 2012, and Kion, where Weichai Power became a key investor in 2013.

This book makes me optimistic that there is huge potential in Chinese–German cooperation. The three cases illustrate clear win-win situations for both sides. I hope that this book is widely read, because a deeper understanding on all sides is a conditio sine qua non for a peaceful and successful development toward Globalia, the globalized world of the future.

Bonn, Germany Hermann Simon

Foreword by Wang Weidong, Minister Counselor of the Economic and Commercial Department of the Chinese Embassy in Germany

2017 marks the 45th year since the establishment of diplomatic relations between China and Germany, which have been growing mature and stable and also have been the leading and stabilizing force between China and Europe in recent years. Like a hybrid sports car with plenty of fuel, strong horsepower, brand new materials, and high speed, the cooperation between China and Germany builds on a solid basis and covers broad areas at high levels, setting a great example for a mutually beneficial cooperation between developing and developed economies. As the Minister Counselor of the Economic and Commercial Department of the Chinese Embassy in Germany, I have the pleasure to witness the profound change in the Chinese–German cooperation in commerce and trade in the last 5 years.

During President Xi's visit to Germany in 2014, a comprehensive strategic partnership between Germany and China was established. One significant indication of this strategic partnership is the ever-growing investment and cooperation between the two countries. As of now, Germany accounts for 40% of the stock of investment from the European Union in China, i.e., more than 70 billion euros, while 5000 German companies created close to 1 million jobs in China. This exemplifies the openness of the Chinese market toward German companies. Meanwhile, Chinese investment in Germany has been growing rapidly and accounts for 40% of the total increment of Chinese investment in Europe over the last 5 years, indicating Germany's attractiveness to Chinese companies. For the first time in 2016, China became Germany's largest trading partner, and it could be partly attributed to the bilateral investment that promotes trade between the two countries.

It is worth noting that the Chinese investment is still at an initial stage and only represents less than 1% of the total foreign direct investment in Germany, clearly out of proportion to the 170 billion euros bilateral trade volume between the two countries. A more balanced bilateral investment between the two countries is not only in Germany's interest but also beneficial for Germany's economic growth. By going through the cases featured in this book, readers can recognize the courage demonstrated by a number of Chinese companies on their paths to globalization. Not only have these companies brought fresh capital, access to the Chinese market, and job opportunities to Germany, they have also enabled the sustainable development of the German counterparts, which would otherwise be facing a bleak outlook.

As China rose to become the world's second largest economy, the rapid growth of Chinese FDI is inevitable in light of China's economic growth and deepening globalization of the Chinese firms. However, some European media and politicians accuse China of being a threat and claim that backed by China's national industrial strategy, the Chinese investors intend to "plunder" the advanced technologies from Europe. Ignoring the difference in the stages of economic development between China and Europe, some of them blame China's restriction on foreign investment in certain areas and demand the Chinese market to be completely open for the sake of "equality." They also claim that the Chinese state-owned enterprises create unfair competition with the help of government subsidies. More often than not, such arguments fail to reflect the reality and cast a wrong and biased image of China onto the German public by treating China's development as a threat. The contribution of the Chinese companies to Germany's economy deserves due respect.

Against this background, this book comes out just in time. Not only can Chinese companies learn from the challenging journey and successful experience in investing in Germany, the German public can also gain a better understanding of the Chinese investors. As the cases presented in this book showcase, the Chinese firms foster a long-term orientation and an open attitude, striving to achieve a mutually beneficial development together with their acquired German firms. And it is because of such mentality and vision, Chinese investors managed to overcome numerous hurdles to help the acquired German firms realize either turnaround or phenomenal growth. I sincerely hope that Germany regards China's rise more as an opportunity than a threat. Speaking of the challenges that result from the competition, I believe the excellent German firms will not fear the competition but take advantage of it to further improve themselves.

Berlin, Germany Wang Weidong

Preface: The Challengers

In January 2008, *The Economist* magazine featured an article entitled "The Challengers" about the rise of multinationals from emerging markets. Now 10 years later, this epithet still appears valid and is an appropriate title for the foreword to a book on Chinese M&A investment in Germany.

Dramatic progress has been made in the years since companies from emerging economies began playing an active role on the global stage. Their voice is growing ever louder, and they are challenging the global dominance of established incumbents. Although we are not able to predict the future, we can gain meaningful insights about probable trends by analyzing past events. To ensure the cogency of our findings, we have conducted an in-depth investigation of three representative cases of mergers and acquisitions (M&As) by Chinese firms in Germany. This book looks beyond the transactions themselves, a topic that has been covered extensively elsewhere. Instead, we are primarily concerned with what happened after the transactions were concluded, in order to address a long list of questions, including: Do M&As create value for shareholders? How do the deals benefit the acquiring company and the company being acquired? Did the German companies change their development paths once the Chinese challengers took the helm?

In the past two decades, a rapidly growing number of Chinese companies have resorted to overseas investments in pursuit of strategic assets and diversification into new regions and industries. Notwithstanding the mixed initial results, as exemplified by early high-profile cross-border investments by Lenovo (formerly known as Legend), TCL, and the like, the enthusiasm of Chinese firms to venture abroad has not subsided. Particularly in recent years, Chinese firms of various sizes and backgrounds have been engaged in internationalization efforts, notably in the form of M&As.

Europe stands out as one of the most important host regions, with Germany being arguably the favorite sovereign market for Chinese investors. China was the biggest source of foreign direct investment (FDI) in Germany in 2015 and 2016, and the number and size of deals are climbing steadily. In the meanwhile, the spectrum of investment targets has expanded to a much wider range of industries, unlike the early years, when the primary focus of Chinese investment in Germany was manufacturing companies. The coming years are expected to see more Chinese M&A activities in Germany. The insights provided by this book can be used to infer Chinese investors' approaches to post-M&A integration and their value creation strategies in Germany as well as in countries outside of Germany.

So far, coverage of this topic by the German media has mainly dealt with the motivation for these M&As and their influence on Germany's labor market, as well as the potential erosion of national sovereignty. Few have looked in depth into the development of these companies, in particular the integration process and subsequent growth post-acquisition. In fact, today's investors are increasingly interested in enhancing the value of their acquired assets.

We used first-hand information to shed light on the endogenous growth model ensuing from M&As. We posit that there are four possible routes to value creation:

- **Traditional post-merger integration**: Combining and reorganizing the businesses of both parties in order to enhance efficiency and gain synergy. This usually includes integrating strategies, systems, organizational structures, human resources, and corporate cultures
- **Expansion in the local market**: Expanding current business in the local market or entering new market segments (categorized by product or geography)
- **Expansion into overseas markets**: Expanding the business to overseas markets by making extensive use of the market experience and local resources of the acquiree/target firm
- **Innovation of business model**: Changing the existing business model, exploring new business areas, and developing innovative products and pricing models

By carrying out M&As in developed economies, investors from emerging economies aim to acquire strategic assets that offer competitive advantages, such as advanced technology, innovative processes, and established brand names. In contrast to their counterparts from the USA, investors from emerging economies, especially China, have recently shown strong preference for the so-called partnering approach during the post-M&A integration period. The partnering approach requires acquiring companies to leave their acquiree's organizational structure largely intact and concentrate on coordinating specific business activities between the acquirer and the acquiree. In effect, the acquiree's incumbent management is entrusted with running the business and enjoys a high level of autonomy. This sort of arrangement is prudent when the Chinese acquirers have inadequate experience in international business management and are less familiar with the environment their newly acquired company operates in. The partnering approach is considered especially helpful for retaining key personnel.

In this book, cases with distinct characteristics were examined in order to provide first-hand information on the impact of these kinds of acquisitions. Some of the companies investigated were state-owned enterprises, while others were privately owned firms. This book's evenhanded analysis will separate the facts from the misconceptions about Chinese investors and will generate useful insights to assist future mergers and acquisitions. We held a series of interviews with senior managers in various functions within the selected organizations to gain additional clarity on their choice of value creation strategies and their subsequent growth patterns by asking them about the following topics:

- Corporate governance after integration
- The short- to medium-term effectiveness of business integration
- Long-term growth road maps and growth drivers

Where applicable, we conducted quantitative analyses, in addition to qualitative interviews, to investigate the financial and operative performance of the Chinese acquirer and German acquiree over time and to validate the findings of the interviews.

We firmly believe that Chinese M&A investment in Germany will continue on its current course for the foreseeable future. This book aims to foster more transparent cooperation and knowledge exchange between Sino-German/European business communities and promote good corporate governance and sustainable growth strategies after M&As.

Cologne, Germany — Jan Y. Yang
Frankfurt am Main, Germany — Lei Chen
Frankfurt am Main, Germany — Zheng Tang

Acknowledgment

The authors would like to thank the three companies in the case studies. In particular, we thank the leadership of ShangGong Europe as well as the SGSB Group, especially Zhang Min, Zheng Ying, Dietrich Eickhoff, and Michael Kilian for their kind support and valuable insights.

The authors would like to express their gratitude to the managers of CIMC and Ziegler for agreeing to participate in this research project and for providing first-hand data and insights to enrich our case study. Special thanks go to Youjun Luan, CEO of Ziegler Group, for making this possible.

We are indebted to Chris Yu and Wang Ziran of Simon-Kucher & Partners and Liang Shuanglin, Feng Yuxuan, and Zuo Wei of China International Investment Promotion Agency (Germany) who also contributed to this book.

Contents

About the Authors

Jan Y. Yang oversees business development and project execution related to the firm's China business. He is based out of Cologne Office and Shanghai Office.

Simon-Kucher & Partners, Strategy & Marketing Consultants, Cologne, Germany

Lei Chen worked for leading consultancies such as Simon-Kucher and KPMG before moving into the industry. He is an expert in topline growth and cross-border M&As. He is based in Düsseldorf and Frankfurt am Main.

Shaangu Europa Forschung und Entwicklung GmbH, Frankfurt am Main, Germany

Zheng Tang served in the commerce department of the Chinese General Consulate in Frankfurt, Germany, before assuming the position in China International Investment Promotion Agency (Germany). He is an expert in bilateral trade and investment between China and Germany.

China International Investment Promotion Agency (Germany), Frankfurt am Main, Germany

Academic Advisor

Hermann Simon is a German business leader and author. Simon co-founded Simon-Kucher & Partners in 1985. From 1995 to 2009, he served as CEO of the company and since then as chairman. Simon is an expert in strategy, marketing, and pricing. He has an extensive global range of clients. In the German-language area, he was voted the most influential management thinker after the late Peter Drucker.

Simon-Kucher & Partner, Strategy and Marketing Consultants, Bonn, Germany

Part I

An Overview of Recent Chinese M&A Activities

Hermann Simon, the most influential management thinker in German-speaking countries after the late Peter Drucker, predicted that the twenty-first century would be the century of Globalia. In today's world, globalization is an imperative. Despite notable setbacks to this process in recent times, globalization is a megatrend that is unlikely to reverse. In order to be successful over the long-term, companies have to be active in the top-tier markets: China, the European Union, and the United States.

Compared to their Western counterparts, Chinese firms significantly lag behind in terms of internationalization. The early movers were not entirely successful due to their lack of experience combined with unfortunate mismanagement. However, this situation is changing. Huawei is frequently cited as a role-model Chinese company that has successfully implemented an internationalization strategy in many parts of the world. Besides the big names, there are also many lesser-known companies playing an active role in the course of globalization. In the export arena, Germany and China are very similar in that small to medium-sized companies are responsible for these two countries' success. About 68% of Chinese exports are manufactured by firms with less than 2000 employees and approximately 70% of German exports come from *Mittelstand* (medium-sized) companies, providing their economies with a hidden champions export turbo (see Fig. 1).

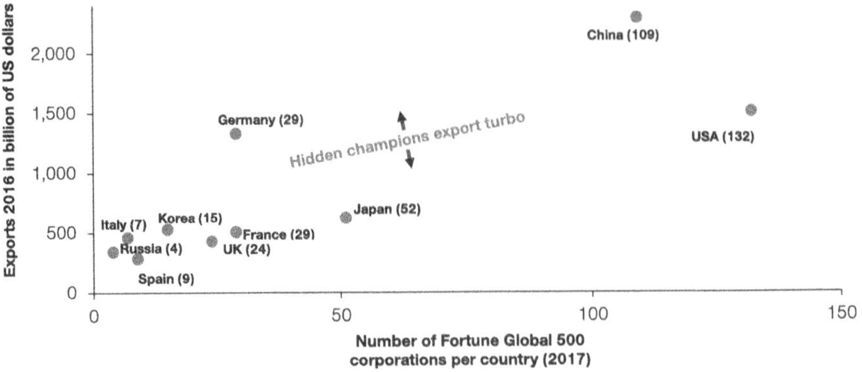

Fig. 1 Export performance of Fortune Global 500 corporations (2015). Source: https://www.destatis.de

With their strong focus on export and extremely high levels of expertise in specific areas, German companies have become attractive targets for Chinese investors seeking for growth opportunities outside of their home country. In this chapter, we will give an account of Chinese M&A activities from recent years before reviewing the historical background of the Chinese companies that have expanded abroad. We will then discuss Germany's status as one of the favorite host regions for Chinese investors as well as the recent trends that have been reshaping the M&A landscape in Germany. To conclude the chapter, we will take stock of the political and legal situations in Germany and China with regard to foreign direct investment.

1 China Goes Global

Before the recent wave of M&A activities from Chinese companies in Germany, there were at least four other major waves of M&As worldwide, beginning with the Americans' expansion into Europe after the World War II. Their international activities were, in turn, followed by similar waves by the Europeans in the 1960s, the Japanese in the 1970s, and finally the Korean and Taiwanese in the 1980s. M&As proved to be a effective vehicle for multinationals to expand overseas.

The new millennium marked a turning point in the global foreign investment landscape as emerging economies started to become active on the world stage. Among others, China accelerated its globalization process considerably through outbound foreign direct investment.

In 2016, with total investment of 218 billion US dollars, China surpassed the United States (189 billion dollars) to become number one in cross-border M&A investment for the first time. That year, China invested more than twice as much as it did in 2015, while US outbound investment decreased by 15%. In addition, China outstripped the United States in terms of average deal size (302 million dollars vs. 131 million dollars).

Chinese governmental support played a pivotal role in propagating the surge of overseas investment. The government has been using its power to cultivate national brands and global players. The central pillar of its strategy is the "Go Global" policy, which encourages Chinese companies to make outward investment. It was initially introduced in 1999 and has evolved over time to include a plethora of other policies enacted at a range of administrative levels, from central government to provincial and even municipal. Qualified investors were given preferential treatment, such as relaxed authorization procedures, financial incentives including tax deductions and low-interest loans, as well as aid in the form of professional services related to overseas investment.

As a result of these incentives, Chinese companies are increasingly setting their sights on global markets. Their cross-border M&As tend to be motivated by the pursuit of strategic assets, such as managerial expertise, international market knowledge, and cutting-edge technology. Acquiring advanced foreign companies affords

J. Y. Yang et al., *Chinese M&As in Germany*, Management for Professionals,
https://doi.org/10.1007/978-3-319-99405-5_1

direct access to intellectual capital that is difficult to obtain without formal governance structures in place.

As strategic assets are the principal goal, it is no surprise that Chinese firms most frequently look to developed economies for M&A targets. Chinese firms show a particular interest in Germany. Although it is a stereotypical perception among Chinese that Germany stands for quality and rigor, there is a factual basis for this belief. Above all, Germany has a well-established manufacturing base, offering investors with varying financial means a broad choice of potential acquisition targets. Many of these manufacturing companies are so-called hidden champions. For the benefit of readers not familiar with the concept, Hermann Simon coined the term in the early 1990s, highlighting the phenonomen of successful, highly specialized small to medium-sized enterprises. These firms are usually undisputed market leaders in their respective industries but are not well known by the public. Interestingly, Germany and other German-speaking countries are a major hub for hidden champions. Furthermore, Germany is known for its research and development (R&D) capabilities on multiple technological fronts and possesses extensive knowledge and expertise regarding Industry 4.0, biopharma, eMobility, to name just a few. All of these areas fall under the category of strategic assets and as such are highly sought after by Chinese firms eager to migrate up the value chain. For this reason, Germany will remain a top destination for Chinese outbound investment for years to come.

Unlike the other goals of foreign direct investment, such as greater efficiency, access to resources and new markets, etc., the impact of strategic asset-seeking acquisitions usually takes longer to become apparent as successfully integrating value-creating assets is much more difficult. Consequently, the authors contend that Chinese investors are unlikely to unlock the full potential of M&A activities in the short run. Not only do the Chinese firms have relatively limited technological capital and innovation capabilities, and lack international experience, they are also constrained by their absorptive capacity, i.e. a firm's ability to recognize the value of new information or knowledge, assimilate and apply it for monetization. With this limitation in mind, it is not uncommon for Chinese investors new to cross-border M&As to adopt a "soft and selective approach" or a "partnering approach" during the post-M&A integration phase. Such approaches typically require the incumbent management to be retained largely intact with only a handful of staff seconded from China to fill specific positions, on a temporary basis in most cases. To the best of our knowledge, most of the Chinese secondees to Germany take on roles related to finance or controlling, or act simply as coordinators to facilitate information flow between Germany and China. As numerous cases have shown, the Chinese representatives tend to refrain from taking an active part in operations, no matter the level of seniority they have in their own organizations. As a matter of fact, they seem content with being recognized as the "bridge guys", sitting behind the scenes, as was often the case with the overseas secondments of Korean multinational firms. Although Chinese managers have only assumed actual general management roles in a small number of cases, the involvement of CEOs of the mother companies has been essential to the success of M&As by Chinese firms in Europe, previous research has found. Details about the involvement of Chinese CEOs have been largely kept out of the public sphere. This book profiles several of these CEOs, whose vision and leadership exert great influence on value creation through M&A's in Germany.

Another intriguing angle that this book tries to explore is the contrast between state-owned enterprises (SOEs) and privately owned companies. Conventional wisdom suggests that unlike SOEs, which have government-controlled resources at their disposal, private firms have to compete based on their technological and marketing capabilities. Moreover, private firms tend to be more effective than SOEs in terms of market orientation and innovation. In addition, private companies have greater flexibility and autonomy in terms of management and decision-making. This implies that private firms may be able to compete more effectively in foreign markets and integrate target firms better than SOEs, leading to higher performance levels overall. Given their differing ownership structures, it is natural that there are differences in how the two types of companies approach post-M&A integration and growth, however, the jury is still out on whether private firms are in fact superior to SOEs.

2 Germany Is a Favored Host Country for Chinese FDI

Cross-border M&A activities by Chinese firms gained steam following the introduction of the "Go Global" policy around the year 2000. However, in the early years, Chinese M&As in Germany were a rarity. They first gained noticeable momentum around 2010 (see Fig. 2.1) when both the number and size of M&A deals were on the rise. Chinese companies took advantage of the weak financial position of European firms, which sped up their penetration into Europe in the aftermath of the global financial crisis.

Germany was the largest recipient of FDI from China in 2016. With 11 billion euros worth of completed deals, Germany accounted for 31% of total Chinese direct investment in Europe. The largest transactions were Midea's acquisition of the robotics maker KUKA (4.5 billion euros); Beijing Enterprises' acquisition of the waste incineration and power generation company EEW Energy (1.4 billion euros); CIC's investment in the German property group BGP (1 billion euros); and China National Chemical Corporation's acquisition of the industrial machinery manufacturer KraussMaffei Group (925 million euros). The size of this increase also meant that, for the first time, annual Chinese FDI flows into Germany were greater than the other way around. This dramatic change in two-way FDI dynamics has become a major subject of policy debates related to Chinese investment.

The surge of investment in Germany coincided with the introduction of wide-ranging fiscal and monetary policies by Chinese authorities. In an attempt to keep GDP growth afloat amid the global financial crisis, the State Council of the People's Republic announced a four trillion yuan stimulus package on November 9, 2008. The size of the stimulus equated to 14% of China's GDP that year. Back then, China's budget deficit was so low that after the stimulus, China's debt amounted to a mere 20% of its GDP. Since then, the People's Bank of China (central bank) has embarked on an expansionary monetary policy, whose effect is still to be felt to this day. In the first half of 2009 alone, bank credit increased by 7.3 trillion yuan, surpassing the original annual target. As a result, the financial market has been flooded with liquidity. Much of this cheap credit has found its way into overseas investment for lack of local investment opportunities, not to mention the relatively high valuation of public companies on stock exchanges in

J. Y. Yang et al., *Chinese M&As in Germany*, Management for Professionals,
https://doi.org/10.1007/978-3-319-99405-5_2

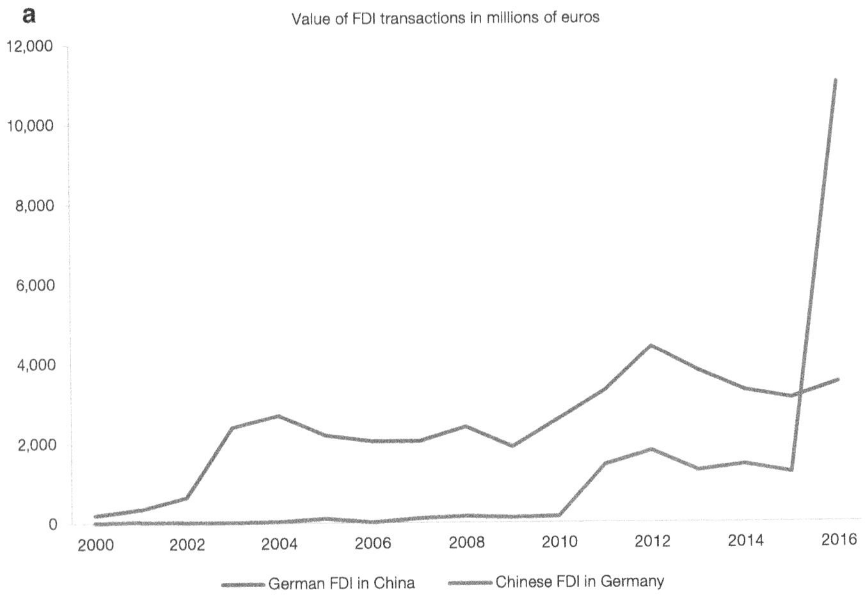

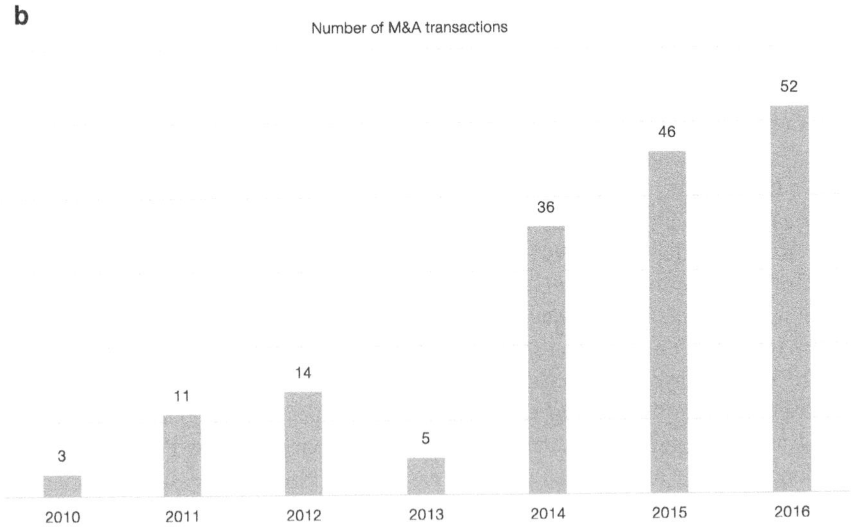

Fig. 2.1 (**a**) Value of FDI transactions (2000–2016). Source: Simon-Kucher; Estimates based on Merics papers on China (January 2017, Rhodium Group). (**b**) Number of M&A transactions by Chinese investors in Germany (2000–2016). Source: M&A China/Deutschland

mainland China, which incentivized the Chinese firms to bring foreign assets onto their balance sheets. Most recently, overseas investment has also been considered an effective hedge against the widely speculated depreciation of the yuan.

Fig. 2.2 Annual GDP growth rate of China (2000–2016)

Outward-looking policies kept China's growth engine running throughout the global financial crisis, while China recorded GDP growth of 10.6% as recently as 2010. However, China's economy has since slowed, most evidently from 2013 onward (see Fig. 2.2). The International Monetary Fund's estimate for the long-term growth rate is around 6%, as the Chinese economy shifts toward consumption and services. Speculation abounds about the possibility of a hard landing once the central government decides to withdraw liquidity. To make matters worse, China is gradually losing its traditional advantage in low-cost manufacturing due to rocketing wage inflation, which has led to production sites being relocated to Southeast Asian countries, such as Vietnam and Bangladesh. Low-end manufacturing industry in China is in severe jeopardy. On a more positive note, the burgeoning middle class has amassed considerable purchasing power and an appetite for high-quality goods. In this context, cross-border M&As present themselves as a sensible choice insofar as the acquired technology and know-how can be transferred back to China to satisfy the changing demand of customers and generate a competitive edge in the high-end market.

Chinese overseas M&As were historically dominated by state-owned enterprises, yet recent years have seen an increasing number of deals led by privately owned companies. This trend is particularly pronounced in the M&A investments of Chinese companies in Germany. Both the number and volume of transactions completed by private-owned enterprises have grown dramatically over the last few years.

The increasing importance of privately owned enterprises in M&A activities in Germany is also underlined by their involvement in certain high-profile deals. Table 2.1 lists some of the most prominent M&A investments by Chinese companies in Germany. Remarkably, 6 out of 12 of the acquirers listed are privately owned.

In terms of their target, Chinese companies have been increasingly favoring "trending" industries, such as smart manufacturing, information transmission, software, and information technology. This is due to industrial restructuring and upgrading, as well as the deployment of Chinese companies' global value chain.

Prior to 2010, seven out of ten Chinese M&A investments in Germany were in industrial manufacturing, especially equipment manufacturing. As the number of

Table 2.1 High profile Chinese M&As in Germany (2016)

Acquiree	Industry	Acquirer	Ownership of acquirer	Value (millions of euro)
KUKA AG (closed in early 2017)	Manufacturing	Midea Group	Private	4500
EEW Energy from Waste GmbH	Energy	Beijing Enterprises Group	State-owned	1411
KraussMaffei Group GmbH	Manufacturing	SinoChem	State-owned	925
Aixtron SE (called off)	Science and technology	Fujian Grand Chip Investment Fund	State-owned	665
Nordic Yards	Manufacturing	Genting Hong Kong Limited	Private	221
TechniSat Automotive	Manufacturing	Ningbo Joyson Electronic	Private	209
Bilfinger SE Water Tech Unit	Manufacturing	Chengdu Tianxiang Environment	Private	90
Manz AG	Science and technology	Shanghai Electric (Group) Corp.	State-owned	–
Medisana AG	Life sciences	Xiamen Comfort Science and Technology (Group) Co.	Private	–
Windmw GmbH	Energy	China Three Gorges Corporation	State-owned	–
Schimmel Pianofortefabrik	Consumer goods	Pearl River Piano Group Co., Ltd.	State-owned	–
Crelux GmbH	Life sciences	Wuxi AppTec	Private	–

Source: Simon-Kucher desk research

Chinese acquiring companies increases, there has been a trend toward diversification into new industries and a gradual move away from manufacturing and automotive spare parts. Industries such as consumer goods and life sciences are becoming more attractive due to increased demand from newly emergent Chinese middle-class consumers (Table 2.2 and Fig. 2.3).

Table 2.2 Number of M&As per industry in Germany (2014–2016)

Year	Auto	Biotechnology	eCommerce	Energy	IT/internet	Consumer goods	Machinery	Recycling	Hotels	Other
2014	11	0	0	4	0	1	8	4	2	6
2015	7	1	1	1	2	6	10	3	2	13
2016	6	4	1	4	4	2	15	2	0	14

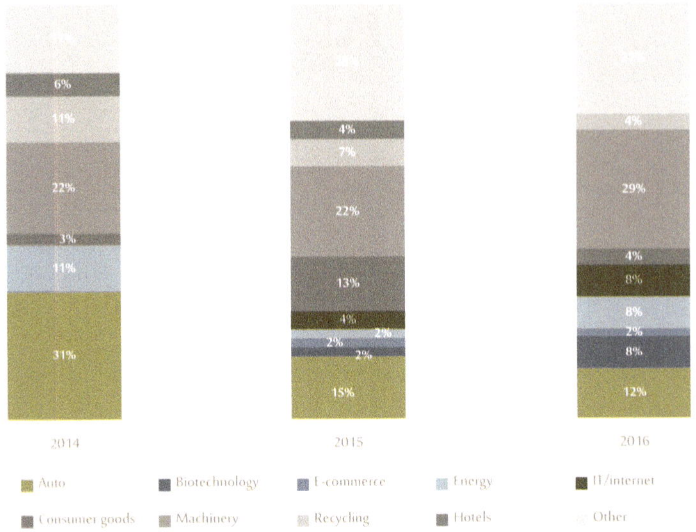

Fig. 2.3 Proportion of M&As per industry in Germany (2014–2016). Source: Simon-Kucher desk research

Overview of General Environment for M&A in Germany

3

Surges of direct investment from a particular country into Europe are nothing new. Each time an FDI "invasion" has occurred, it has caused unrest both at a governmental level, due to concerns about the loss of national sovereignty, and at the local level among companies concerned about the competitive threat by the supposed interlopers. In the 1960s–1970s, it was mainly US investors that settled in the newly created customs union of the European Economic Community (EEC). With their superior technological and organizational skills, US firms were once predicted to sweep out domestic companies. The initial opposition to the US investors lessened after, as local firms often managed to absorb technology and know-how from their US competitors and that the impact on employment and research activities was mostly positive.

European governments and corporates were equally skeptical when Japanese and Korean companies were attracted to the growing European common market in the 1980s–1990s in order to avoid its common external tariff. The Japanese were considered a particularly serious threat to German manufacturers. Japanese car manufacturers were beating the major German players in their export markets and even in Germany itself thanks to their superior production technology combined with a good cost-performance ratio. In other industries, such as photography, electronics, and optics, it was even worse for the local firms. Japanese competitors wiped out many well-established German brands. However, to put things in perspective, the investment of those Japanese manufacturers in Germany was insignificant compared to their import volumes.

It was a tough wake-up call for German industry, which had previously only benefited from globalization and trade. Since the early 1950s, Germany had been taking advantage of relatively cheap skilled labor and open markets for its exports, especially the USA and the UK. With rising labor costs and declining innovation in the 1970s, Germany gradually lost its competitiveness.

In this context, one might have expected the German government to introduce protectionist economic policies. However, the argument that open markets were beneficial to the German economy prevailed and an open investment policy was maintained. This position was strengthened by further European integration, a project

J. Y. Yang et al., *Chinese M&As in Germany*, Management for Professionals,
https://doi.org/10.1007/978-3-319-99405-5_3

based on a belief in free markets. Therefore, the call for protecting German industry from international competition and building up barriers against foreign investors never gained significant traction.

More often than not, Chinese investors target German firms with advanced technological reserves but troubled finances. This not only means a moderate price tag on those entities but also alludes to low expectations on the German side. Usually, the central question is whether the investor will keep the acquired firm going as a viable concern and retain a significant number of jobs. In deals of this kind, the Chinese investors have little to lose, as if worst comes to worst, the investor only has to cash out on its acquired assets. Nevertheless, the upside potential for the investor is enormous. The technology it acquires can be deployed in China and the newly acquired entity can be used as a platform to sell its "Made in China" products in the European market, while expensive parts manufactured in Germany can be replaced with parts from China at lower cost.

Another factor is also contributing to the generally positive sentiment Chinese have toward Germany. The mid-sized, often family-owned businesses that form the backbone of the German economy tend to focus their activities on relatively small niches and strive for market leadership in these narrow segments—a strategy that requires them to define the whole world as their target market in order to be successful. As China's economy is still growing rapidly, it has a huge appetite for the products these companies make and we have seen a steady increase in trade volumes from Germany to China.

Chinese investment in Germany still has a lot of catching up to do. It was only in late 2016 and early 2017 that the volume of investments from China to Germany increased to such an extent that the wider public took serious notice. However, this will only be passing phase for two reasons. First, the fervor of Chinese investors has cooled due to restrictions imposed by the Chinese government on overseas investments in a bid to promote the strategic selection of targets and discourage speculation-driven financial investments, especially those with high levels of leverage. Second, the Trump administration has made its view on free trade clear and has been vocal in criticizing the USA's trade deficit with Germany. Despite declarations from the Chinese government stressing the advantages of free trade, it is understandable that questions arise about how level the playing fields actually are. In this context, it remains to be seen whether Germany can rely on the US remaining a net customer of German goods. It may be pragmatic for Germany to seek new partners to compensate for this potential loss in trade volume.

4 European and German Controls on Foreign Direct Investment

Germany has a sound legal system and offers a reasonable policy environment for acquisitions by foreign companies. According to German law, approval is needed for M&As in specific industries. In the military industry, for example, acquisitions to take ownership of more than a 25% stake in a company have to be assessed and authorized by the German government. It is necessary to make a declaration when acquiring stakes of 10% or more in banks and financial service companies and approval is needed from the financial service authority. There are similar regulations in the insurance industry. Assets transfers (not ownership transfers) in the sectors energy supply, telecommunications, transportation, natural resource exploitation, chemicals, and construction require approval from government authorities. German law also dictates that assessments have to be carried out for acquisitions of listed companies or any firm that has a significant impact on its industry.

4.1 European Merger Regulation

The key objective of the EU Merger Regulation is to maintain effective competition and develop the common market. By the end of April 2017, 5228 mergers had been audited, of which 24 mergers were rejected based on the Merger Regulation. It is important to note that mergers (legal and financial mergers) are distinct from controlling acquisitions (sole or joint control).

For M&As that would result in a controlling interest, revenue thresholds are a determining factor. If the annual revenue of all the enterprises involved totals 5 billion euros for the financial year, the enterprises have to notify the European Commission about the merger. In addition, the Commission has to review the significance of the amalgamation and a forecast of future market conditions is made. Market dynamics, as well as technical and legal developments, are also taken into consideration. In this context, a distinction is made between product markets and geographic markets.

J. Y. Yang et al., *Chinese M&As in Germany*, Management for Professionals,
https://doi.org/10.1007/978-3-319-99405-5_4

Mergers that fall under the EU Merger Regulation must be registered, examined, and approved by the Commission. A preliminary review is conducted in which the Commission analyzes whether the merger is compatible with the market. If it is not possible to approve the transaction immediately, an in-depth evaluation is conducted, which the Commission uses as a basis to make its final decision on whether or not the firm is market-compatible. The in-depth evaluation has to take place within 90 days of the merger being registered. A merger notification cannot not be given before a clearance decision has been made as part of either the preliminary or in-depth reviews.

4.2 German Merger Controls

If the transaction does not come under the jurisdiction of the European Commission, because either the sales thresholds or the definitions set by the EU Merger Regulation are not met, the merger must also be assessed to determine whether it needs to be registered in an EU member state.

Compared to the EU Merger Regulation, German merger controls apply to a wider range of transactions as they set lower revenue thresholds. In Germany, the threshold is 500 million euros combined annual revenue. However, the first participating company must generate revenue of at least 25 million euros in Germany and the second company must generate over 5 million euros for German merger controls to apply.

Any M&A transaction that reaches this threshold value must comply with the acquisition regulations of the ARC (Act against Restraints of Competition). This means that the transaction cannot be completed until the Germany's federal cartel office has examined the merger. This review is very similar to the review carried out by the European Commission.

In the initial review, the German cartel office has 1 month to determine whether a detailed review of the plan is necessary. If the cartel office finds the merger to be acceptable, it informs the enterprise with a non-contestable declaration. If the cartel office has any reason for concern, it will initiate further a review and inform the enterprise via an administrative notice. The cartel office must make a decision within 4 months of the company being registered, irrespective of whether the merger is accepted or not. In rare circumstances, the Ministry of Economics may overrule an unfavorable decision by the cartel office, thereby authorizing the merger. However, if the cartel office has approved a transaction, the Ministry is unable to overrule the cartel office's decision.

Acknowledgement Special thanks go to Robert Binder, Partner at Warth & Klein Grant Thornton, for his valuable contribution to this topic.

Part II

Case Studies

This chapter presents three case studies, which constitute the most important part of the book. We present first-hand information based on interviews with key stakeholders and data provided by the participating companies. Where appropriate, we also refer to publicly available third-party information, for example, from previous interviews, books, and other sources of interest. Although representatives of the participating companies have reviewed the cases, we cannot guarantee the absolute accuracy of all statements.

The case studies are intended for a broad general-interest readership. As such, the authors endeavor to write in plain language and spare the readers trivial details that are likely to only be of interest to a limited number of individuals with specific background knowledge.

Table 1 Key facts about the cases featured in this book

			Acquired			Annual sales in m€	
Target firm	Industry	Previous owner	in ...	by ...	Acquirer's status	Upon acquisition	FY 2016
Dürkopp Adler (ShangGong Europe)	Industrial sewing machine	Schaeffler	2005	SGSB	State-owned enterprise	102	182[a]
Preh	Automotive electronics	DBAG (PE)	2011	Joyson electronics	Private	412	1176[a]
Ziegler	Fire-fighting equipment	Insolvency	2013	CIMC	State-owned enterprise	168	220

[a]Including sales through acquisitions

The individual cases are presented in the same sequence as in the table above (alphabetic order).

5 ShangGong Europe: The Odyssey of a State-Owned Chinese Enterprise to the West

This case study was published with kind permission of the SGSB Group.

"Das gibt's doch gar nicht" (In English: "That doesn't even exist")

In 1994, a satirical conspiracy theory spread virally on the nascent internet that the city of Bielefeld doesn't actually exist. This is likely still the most well-known anecdote among locals. When Zheng Ying left metropolitan Shanghai and found herself in rustic Bielefeld more than a decade ago, she probably did not realize that it was just the beginning of a long journey for her and her employer, the SGSB Group, which had acquired Dürkopp Adler (DA) from Fischers Aktien Gesellschaft (FAG) in 2005.

People familiar with the matter said it had been a bold move for SGSB. In fact, it was the first time that a Chinese firm had ever acquired a German public company and, strikingly, neither company was in particularly good shape. The SGSB Group was a brand-new company established at the end of 2004 out of a merger between two state-owned enterprises (SOE's): ShangGong (a pinyin abbreviation for Shanghai Industrial Sewing Machine Company) and SMPIC (Shanghai Movie and Photo Industry Corporation). Zhang Min, who used to be the general manager of SMPIC, was appointed chairman and CEO of the merged company. It was not a job that anyone would envy. Like many companies founded in the era of the planned economy, the SGSB Group was struggling against fierce competition from both ends of the market, i.e. low-cost local players and premium foreign brands. Its back was against the wall. It was rumored that if the management team could not find a quick solution to turn the state-owned company around, SGSB was set to be downsized materially. The salvage turned out to be the acquisition of a foreign company thousands of miles away. As a matter of a fact, ShangGong had already been in discussion with DA before SGSB had even been set up.

DA was a German medium-sized company looking back on over 100 years of history. The revered Dürkopp Adler brand had such a solid reputation in the industrial

J. Y. Yang et al., *Chinese M&As in Germany*, Management for Professionals,
https://doi.org/10.1007/978-3-319-99405-5_5

sewing machine sector as comparable to that of BMW or Mercedes in the automotive industry. However, the golden days were long gone by the turn of the twenty-first century as the downstream market started to tumble. The core European markets were, at best, stagnating. To make things worse, premium brands had begun relocating production to low-cost regions in Asia, particularly China. High-end sewing machine producers were no longer competitive and their very existence was in danger. Pessimists believed the European sewing machine sector was doomed.

When the acquisition took place, both parties in the transaction were ailing. Zhang, CEO of the SGSB Group, intentionally kept a low profile, referring to the acquisition as a matter of survival. Twelve years later, the SGSB Group has not only survived against all odds, business is thriving. Its market capitalization increased eightfold from 2005 to 2017, while DA's market value grew by more than ten times in the same period. The weak–weak situation was turned into an exemplary win–win situation. However, it has not been an easy win. There have been plenty of ups and downs down the road, particularly in the aftermath of the global financial crisis around 2008/2009, when DA almost went under—but together, SGSB and DA made it through.

After absorbing DA in 2005 and navigating the difficult waters of the crisis, SGSB acquired Pfaff and KSL in 2013, and Stoll in 2015, all well-known German companies in the sewing machinery sector. Within 12 years, the SGSB Group had become a global powerhouse in industrial sewing machines. Today, its customer base includes nearly every European luxury brand. It sews 90% of all the world's high-end car seats and provides Chinese aircraft manufacturers with 3D-sewing solutions for the composite parts. The company is now actively preparing for the future with the development of sewing robots and smart sewing units in line with the concept of Industry 4.0, among other innovations in its product pipeline.

5.1 Background

Despite all the obvious differences between SGSB and DA, the two parties of the Sino-German partnership had at least one thing in common—they were both the product of their respective historical growth paths.

The SGSB Group's name originates from its two predecessors, ShangGong (Shanghai Industrial Sewing Machine Company) and SMPIC (Shanghai Movie and Photo Industry Corporation). "SG" stands for ShangGong and "SB" is the acronym of ShenBei, the approximate pronunciation of "SMPIC" in Chinese Pidgin English.

Both companies had had their glory days long before the deal took place. ShangGong was the first sewing machine company to be publicly listed in China. Its stocks started trading on the Shanghai Stocks Exchange in September 1993. Under its previous name, the Shanghai Industrial Sewing Machine Factory, the company laid the foundations of its first factory in October 1965. In August 1997, the company was renamed ShangGong Holding Co., Ltd. From the end of 2000, ShangGong's portfolio also included well-known sewing machine brands for household use, such as Butterfly, Flyman, and Bee.

In 2004, ownership of ShangGong was transferred from the light industry system to the Pudong New Area State-owned Assets Supervision and Administration Commission as part of a large program to restructure state-owned assets. SMPIC's assets were integrated into ShangGong, giving rise to the SGSB Group. Zhang, who used to work for SMPIC, was appointed chairman and CEO of the newly formed company.

SMPIC underwent restructuring and repositioning several times before being merged with ShangGong. The predecessor of SMPIC, Shanghai Copier Factory, made China's first domestically produced copier in 1964. The Shanghai Movie and Photo Industry Corporation was officially founded in 1973. Fourteen years later, the company was rebranded as SMPIC. Today, this brand is mainly used for office equipment, which constitutes the bulk of SMPIC's current business. It was also one of the first SOE's to form joint ventures with foreign multinational corporations. In the late 1980s, SMPIC and Xerox established Shanghai Xerox Co., Ltd., to manufacture and market copiers. Today, under the umbrella of SGSB, SMPIC is engaged in trading office stationery, and electronic goods and equipment, in addition to manufacturing and marketing its own-brand office equipment.

At the turn of the twenty-first century, after 20 years of liberalization and reform in China, the SGSB Group, like many of its peer SOE's, found itself suddenly surrounded by a large number of newcomers. Domestic sewing machine suppliers had sprung up like bamboo shoots after the rain. As these competitors were almost all private companies free from the payroll burden of SOE's, they enjoyed a significant cost advantage and won over many price-sensitive customers. In addition, more and more foreign companies were entering China, devouring the higher end of the market. As a result, many SOE's were forced to search for new directions and often had to downsize, costing huge numbers of employees their livings. Forced layoffs reached their peak toward the end of the twentieth century. It was a harsh time for many ordinary Chinese households as well as for state-owned businesses, and the SGSB Group was not immune to these adversities. Once the uncontested market leader in the sewing machine industry in China, ShangGong was pushed out of the top ten in the early 2000s (see Fig. 5.1 for a brief history of the SGSB Group before it started Cross-border M&A's in 2005).

Like SGSB, Dürkopp Adler was originally two independent companies, both of which were founded at about the same time, over a 100 years ago, in the city of Bielefeld in Germany. In the mid-nineteen century, the German sewing machine market was dominated by imports from the USA, which were not only expensive but also difficult to maintain. Two mechanics, Baer and Koch, realizing this might be an business opportunity, started to produce sewing machines at their factory in Bielefeld in 1860. This was the first sewing machine factory in the city.

In 1865, Koch hired two new mechanics, Dürkopp and Schmidt, when Baer left the company to pursue other business opportunities. Dürkopp had designed his first sewing machine back in 1861. He and Schmidt founded Dürkopp & Schmidt in 1867, but the two founders also parted ways later on.

In the 1880s, competition from national and international suppliers grew fierce, as Germany's production capacity for sewing machines at the time almost equaled total

Fig. 5.1 Milestones of the SGSB Group (1965–2005). Source: SGSB Group

worldwide demand. The business prospects for sewing machines were bleak. Dürkopp & Co., as the company was called after Schmidt's departure, began making bicycles like some of its competitors did in Bielefeld. The bicycle manufacturing business took off. Delighted by the success of the initial diversification, Dürkopp & Co., expanded into manufacturing cars and trucks. This endeavor was not particularly successful and Dürkopp had to cease vehicle production in the aftermath of the global economic crisis of the 1920s. Today, prototypes of Dürkopp bicycles and motor vehicles are exhibited at DA's premises in Bielefeld.

In 1962, FAG Kugelfischer, an industrial conglomerate, whose core business was manufacturing bearings, acquired the majority of equity shares in Dürkoppwerke AG (formerly Dürkopp & Co.). Twenty-five years later, the acquirer also took over the majority of shares in Koch's Adler AG, paving the way for a merger of the long-lasting rivals. From 1990 onward, the two companies were based at new facilities in the Oldentrup district of Bielefeld under the name Dürkopp Adler AG. Then in 2001, FAG itself was absorbed by INA-Schaeffler in a hostile takeover.

As one of the leading sewing machine manufacturers worldwide, DA had advanced technological know-how and its namesake brand was well recognized

1860	H. Koch and K. Baer found Bielefeld's first sewing machine factory, later known as Koch & Co.
1867	Dürkopp & Schmidt sewing machine factory founded in Bielefeld
1885	Koch & Co begins manufacturing bicycles, 10 years before Dürkopp & Schmidt starts its own bicycle production
1913	Dürkopp & Schmidt reorganized as Dürkoppwerke AG; Koch & Co. reorganized as Koch's Adler Nähmaschinenwerke AG with Adler as its trademark
1962	FAG Kugelfischer becomes major shareholder of Dürkoppwerke
1971	Koch's Adler reorganized as Koch Adler AG
1986	FAG Kugelfischer becomes the largest shareholder of Koch Adler
1990	Dürkoppwerke merges with Koch Adler to become Dürkopp Adler AG
2001	FAG acquired by INA Schaeffler, which becomes the new owner of Dürkopp Adler AG
2005	Dürkopp Adler AG acquired by the SGSB Group

Fig. 5.2 Milestones of DA (1860–2005). Source: Dürkopp Adler

and trusted by demanding clientele. Nevertheless, it missed the ship when the growth engine of the downstream industry shifted from Western countries to Asia. As a consequence, sales dropped significantly year after year. DA made approximately 150 million euros in revenue with its core sewing machine business in 2001. Four years later, revenue had shrunk to around 100 million euros. DA's production sites were insufficiently coordinated, synergy between its various plants was not tapped, and the company had more employees than work. Management issues and the deteriorating market situation caused DA to make losses for several years in a row.

Once the jewel in the crown, DA had become a headache for its holding company FAG (owned by Schaeffler since the early 2000s) and it was not enthusiastic about increasing investment in the business in order to revive it. After all, sewing machinery had little relevance for the industrial conglomerate's main business. Finding a buyer for DA seemed to be a logical choice for Schaeffler and it would probably benefit DA in the long run, provided the new owner was willing to invest and develop the DA brand (see Fig. 5.2 for a brief history of DA).

5.2 Motivation and Strategy

By the time Zhang joined SGSB from SMPIC, ShangGong had already signed a letter of intent with FAG to acquire DA and the term sheets had been largely determined. However, concerns remained. Would SGSB be able to carry forward the German operations with Chinese managers? Would the German employees be willing to cooperate with the Chinese shareholder? Was it going to be possible for

SGSB to absorb the advanced technology and eventually integrate the German brand?

The ShangGong Group had been struggling for years in a row and it was clear that ShangGong did not stand a chance of defeating the horde of private sewing machine companies in a price war due to its unfavorable cost structure. Sales turnover had halved within few years as competition escalated. In the meantime, ShangGong lacked the technology necessary to compete with foreign players, leaving the company in a precarious situation. ShangGong's management was caught in a painful dilemma: either throw in the towel and exit the sewing machine business entirely, which would make massive layoffs unavoidable, or double down and acquire the advanced technology and know-how it needed to step up the company's core competencies. The fastest way to realize the latter was through a merger or acquisition. No wonder when Ni Yonggang, chairman of ShangGong, learned about FAG's intention to liquidate all of its investment in DA, he was more than eager to strike the deal.

In October 2002, ShangGong submitted an application to the China Securities Regulatory Commission to issue an additional 100 million B shares. The stated purpose of the fund-raising was to acquire DA jointly with another SOE, the Shanghai Tire Rubber Group, and develop special sewing machines based on DA's technology. It took the regulator over a year to approve the application. Shortly thereafter, ShangGong's intended partner, Shanghai Tire Rubber Group, decided to drop out, leaving ShangGong as the sole buyer.

There were also different opinions from within the group about whether the acquisition of DA would be a blessing or a curse for SGSB. Would it make sense to spend tens of millions of euros on a loss-making company? Why would two ailing companies be better off together? Would not it be wiser to invest the money in some safer choices in China? After thorough research and evaluation of all the options, Zhang decided to side with Ni's recommendation based on the belief that demand for clothing, bags, and similar products would not diminish in future. Consequently, there must be growth potential for upstream sewing equipment as it is difficult to replace with other applications. However, SGSB needed to change its modus vivendi. Doing nothing would be nothing less than a suspended death sentence. In order to survive and capture the growth potential, the company would have to overhaul its R&D capabilities and refocus on innovation and higher-end customers. However, he knew it would be difficult from the beginning: "It's like fighting boxing match; there is always a risk, but as long as there is still a chance of winning, I have to go at it." Zhang put his career at stake, as he tried to persuade the board and governmental officials to endorse the deal. When he was given the greenlight internally, he found the negotiations with the Germans had come to a standstill. The atmosphere at the negotiation table was tense. He had to step in and play a more active role to bring the talks back on track.

On the May 3, 2004, the efforts came to fruition. Representatives of ShangGong and FAG signed the letter of intent in the presence of German Chancellor Gerhard Schröder and Chinese Prime Minister Wen Jiabao during his state visit to Germany. It then took several months to complete all paperwork. In the middle of 2005, after nearly 3 years, the deal was finally closed. FAG transferred 94.48% of its DA shares to SGSB. The initial investment in the acquisition was approximately 37 million euros, of which 950,000 euros was to acquire DA's shares and 9 million euros was to pay back the loans made to DA by FAG's shareholders, with the remaining 27 million euros provided as a shareholder loan to be used as working capital. Unfortunately, the initiator of the groundbreaking acquisition, Ni Yonggang, former chairman of the ShangGong Group, passed away before the deal was closed.

Earlier that year, ShangGong had set up a holding platform in Germany, ShangGong (Europe) Holding Corporation GmbH. At the time, ShangGong Europe was, in essence, a shell company established for the sole purpose of acquiring DA. The arrangement was more secure for the seller FAG from a legal point of view as the actual acquiring entity was incorporated in Germany. For SGSB, this set-up was disadvantageous in terms of profit repatriation and tax optimization due to the added layer between the holding company and DA.

According to sources familiar with the matter, prior to the takeover, there was a vague plan at most about what to do with the combined business. Ni might have had a master plan in his head, but there were no written documents whatsoever. After signing the deal on October 29, 2014, Zhang put forward a business plan based on the market due diligence exercise that aimed to increase enterprise value through layoffs and by relocating production, but fundamentally, there was no strategic planning beyond that.

5.3 Integration and Transformation

According to Chinese tradition, 12 years constitute a cycle. SGSB spearheaded its overseas operations exactly 12 years ago with the acquisition of DA. When asked about the milestones during the last 12 years, Zhang named three important phases. The first 3 years were a warm-up phase for both parties to get acquainted with each other and build trust. Integration efforts centered on improving efficiency. At the end of the first phase, DA was confronted with immense top-line challenges amid the financial crisis. The company was on the verge of bankruptcy as liquidity was almost drained. Nevertheless, DA managed to escape catastrophe thanks to financial aid from the Chinese holding company. In 2013, SGSB and DA entered a completely new era. Pfaff, the direct competitor of DA, was bailed out of bankruptcy by ShangGong Europe and the two firms came under the same roof. SGSB then acquired two more innovative German companies in a very short period of time. Consequently, ShangGong Europe emerged as a holding company with greater operating responsibilities and a high-profile brand portfolio.

5.3.1 Phase 1 (2005–2008): The Moment of Truth—The Chinese Came to Town

The transfer of ownership was now official. In the middle of 2005, the SGSB Group took over nearly 95% of DA's shares and thus became its majority shareholder. It was a seminal moment. For the first time, a Chinese state-owned enterprise had taken over a publicly traded German company. Expectation was high on both sides, as was the uncertainty about how—by joining together—the two companies would escape the downward spiral, create value for the shareholders, and provide job security to the employees in Bielefeld and elsewhere.

The burden to find an adequate solution fell upon the new owner SGSB. The excitement about acquiring a well-known foreign company ebbed away quickly after the deal was closed. The SGSB Group now had to articulate its master plan and find its own solutions to the many challenges that were arising as integration progressed. There were practically no precedents to learn from, and no one within the state-owned organization had experience in dealing with, let alone managing, foreign subsidiaries. Although SGSB used to work with foreign companies, such as Juki from Japan and Singer from the United States, it used to be limited to operational cooperation and was therefore the experience not particularly helpful in the case of DA.

SGSB's management was convinced from the outset that the potential synergy between SGSB and DA was immense. Nevertheless, tapping that synergy was a daunting task. Probably the most difficult part lay in figuring out how to bring across the expectations and vision of the Chinese shareholder to the German workforce. If they did not consider themselves part of the SGSB Group and failed to realize that their interests were closely tied to those of SGSB, the integration would be doomed to failure. One most dreaded scenario of the local employees was that the Chinese were only interested in DA's technology and brand, and that they would abandon the German operations, as soon as they achieved their goal, slashing jobs down the road. In the previous 10 years, layoffs had become sort of routine at DA under FAG Kugelfischer's ownership. The headquarters in Bielefeld used to employ 2500 people at its peak. Just before the takeover, only about 450 people were working there and the company had been making losses for several consecutive years. Staff morale was reasonably low, as the uncertainty with a new owner from the "Middle Kingdom" was just as large.

Immediately after the acquisition, DA employees were assured that Bielefeld would remain the center for marketing, R&D, and manufacturing of high-end equipment. In order to demystify SGSB's agenda, Zhang went to great lengths to communicate with the German team and reassure them that SGSB was committed to investing in DA and intended to take it to the next level. Not only did SGSB stand to benefit from the acquisition, DA would also have an unprecedented growth opportunity. To make sure that his message was fully understood, he even conducted one-on-one conversations with middle-level management. This was not something the CEO of an acquiring company would typically do following an acquisition. Looking back, Zhang believes this approach helped stabilize the mood and instill confidence within the team.

In contrast to the SGSB Group, DA's staff had more experience in working with foreign colleagues. DA had been producing in the Czech Republic and Romania for several years, making the Bielefeld employees relatively open to new things, under circumstances, even a new employer. Zhang recalls that the German staff had a lot of ideas and their professional ethics were impeccable. As the Chinese investors acted with integrity and lived up to their word, it did not take long for the German staff to put aside their concerns about the company's intentions and embrace the common goal of driving both companies back onto a growth path.

However, there was still noticeable skepticism about SGSB's capability to lead the traditional German firm with over 100 years' history. This was understandable to the extent that the investor from Shanghai was not in a good shape and had no advantage whatsoever over DA. SGSB was clearly lagging behind, particularly in terms of technological know-how and brand equity. Aware of its own weaknesses, the SGSB leadership was mindful to not micromanage the newly acquired German subsidiary. The incumbent management team at DA was largely retained, including CEO Werner Heer. The only representative SGSB sent to join the management board in Bielefeld was Ms. Zheng Ying. As chairman of the supervisory board, Zhang would meet Heer, head of the management board, on a regular basis to discuss DA's strategic direction. A lean management model was devised and implemented. At an operational level, Heer focused on the front-end and was in charge of production, R&D, sales and marketing, while his Chinese colleague Zheng was responsible for finance, personnel, and IT. In addition, Zheng served as the liaison officer between the SGSB Group and DA to make sure a smooth and timely exchange of information.

Once the managerial structure had been settled, the new DA management team wasted no time in taking a series of measures to overhaul the distressed company. Commercial policy was among the first to be tackled. Purchase orders with extensive account receivables were deprioritized or turned down at all and inventory was trimmed to free up liquidity. Production planning was streamlined too. In the past, all components had been made in Germany. DA's management reassessed the manufacturing value chain, reshuffling it to better realize economy of scale across factories. Following the changes, the site at Minerva Boskovice in the Czech Republic was primarily tasked with in manufacturing medium- to heavy-duty machines, while the second European production site outside Germany, located in Sangeorgiu de Mures, Romania, was tasked with producing Dürkopp Adler-brand components and spare parts for automatic sewing machines, especially mechanical parts requiring labor-intensive work. The headquarters in Bielefeld would continue to focus on DA's overall market strategy, new product development, and the assembly of high-end sewing equipment.

SGSB instructed DA management to cut expenditure on administration, sales and marketing, literally everywhere possible, except for R&D. It was clear to Zhang that in order to revive DA and save SGSB, it was crucial to maintain a competitive edge on technology. Even in the most difficult of times, SGSB stuck unrelentingly to this principle. Dietrich Eickhoff, former spokesperson of the management board at DA and now managing director of ShangGong Europe, credits much of DA's success today to the Chinese owner's determination to continue investing in technology and people.

The first year after the acquisition ended just well. Although full-year revenue declined by 9% in 2005 from the previous year, DA had returned to profitability. As a token of appreciation and celebration of this initial success, the Chinese shareholder distributed a special Christmas bonus of 300 euro for every employee in

Germany, which was unheard of in DA's history. In response, the president of the works council sent a letter of thanks on behalf of the workforce.

In 2006, DA succeeded in growing its top-line again, generating 13% higher revenue. Also that year, DA started to get a foothold in China. In April, a joint sales company was established between SGSB (60%) and DA (40%) to market DA brands and serve local customers. In August, a manufacturing company was founded to take over part of the manufacture of DA's standard sewing machines at the Romanian factory.

Despite the successful start, the supervisory board decided to part ways with CEO Werner Heer by the end of the year, citing irreconcilable differences of opinions. He remained on the management board until the end of November 2006, while Alfred Wadle succeeded him as the spokesperson for the management board from September 1, 2006. Wadle had been with DA in different functions for a long time. Among others, he used to head the Czech subsidiary of DA and belonged to the few persons at DA with rich experience in managing an international company with stakeholders of different cultural backgrounds. He was considered an ideal successor, more importantly, because he identified with the strategic direction of the Chinese shareholder. Soon after Wadle took office, he started to strengthen cooperation with China, including sourcing spare parts partially from China, among others.

Under Wadle's stewardship, DA performed satisfactorily, on par with 2006 in terms of revenue and profitability. However, weakening demand could already be sensed and portended a widespread economic downturn amid the global financial crisis. In the 2008 financial year, DA's revenue plunged by 20%, while operating profit dropped by more than 50% (see Fig. 5.3).

5.3.2 Phase 2 (2009–2012): Live or Die—DA Rebounds in the Aftermath of the Global Financial Crisis

It was the best and the worst of times. Three years after the acquisition, the Chinese and the German teams had gradually found an effective way to work with each other, as the integration process continued. The company had a healthy product development pipeline and looked to new opportunities in China and other fast-growing countries with the support of the Chinese shareholder. It was at this point when the global financial crisis hit. The future of DA was put on a knife-edge. SGSB played a decisive role in saving the German hidden champion from its demise. Even in the very depths of the crisis, Zhang stressed time and again publicly that SGSB would not give up on Bielefeld.

When the subprime mortgage bubble burst in the United States in 2007, the crisis that followed had a ripple effect across many different parts of the world, leading to a global economic downturn. In the aftermath, continental Europe was caught in the middle of a severe sovereign debt crisis. If the year 2008 was bad for business, 2009 was catastrophic for DA and the entire industry. The main players in sewing machine industry around the world, including the Japanese powerhouses, Juki and Brother, and the major Chinese sewing machine manufacturers, all suffered as sales fell by more than 40% on average.

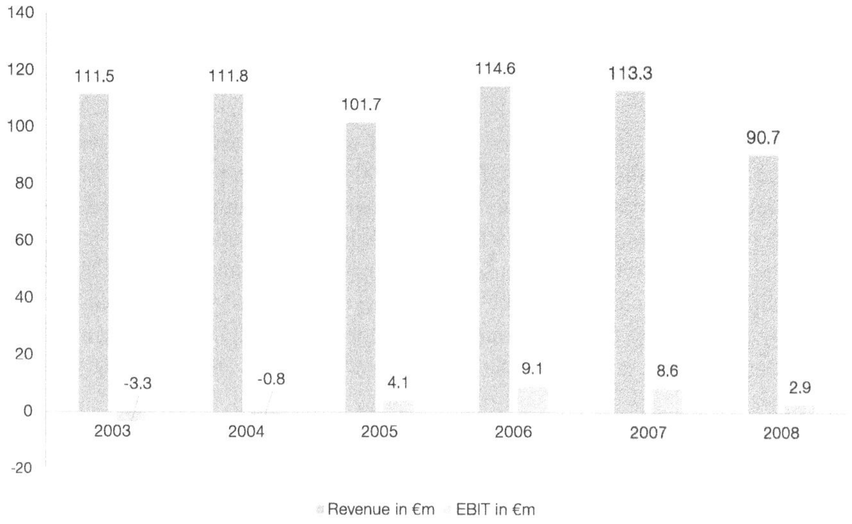

Fig. 5.3 DA's revenue and EBIT (2003–2008). Source: ShangGong Europe

> Only when the tide goes out do you discover who's been swimming naked.—Warren Buffet

Commenting on that difficult period, Eickhoff noted that DA had missed out on the textile boom in China. With the Chinese investor on board, one would expect acceleration of strategic deployment in China. Unfortunately, before any efforts could materialize, significant and continuous cost increases in China led to a massive migration of the garment industry to neighboring countries, which, in turn, triggered the closure of tens of thousands of Chinese factories. At DA, sales and marketing were not up to the same high standard as its technology. DA's sales in Southeast Asia, the fastest-growing area for sewing machines, had actually been declining for years.

In 2009, total sewing machines sales for DA fell by 43% to 51.8 million euros (or by 55% compared to before the crisis) and earnings before interest and tax (EBIT) plummeted to a loss of 18.4 million euros. Weighing the changes in the external environment and the challenges within the organization, Zhang made amends with Heer, the former CEO, who returned as spokesperson of the management board in May 2009. According to Heer, it would take a series of emergency measures and a lot of good luck to get out of the crisis.

Within a short time frame, DA realized a cost reduction of 18.3 million euros, primarily by laying off 515 employees across the company. SGSB waived 12 million euros worth of shareholder loans, thereby narrowing down the capital deficit to 21.2 million euros. It was one of the turning points in DA's history. Although Zhang had gone on record several times to express his commitment to Bielefeld, it was not until he provided this crucial financial aid that he definitively convinced the German employees of his sincerity. Thanks to SGSB's intervention, the former majority shareholder FAG Kugelfischer also agreed to forego a debt of 5.5 million euros.

Unfortunately, all these measures were still not enough to prevent DA from having to sell its profitable subsidiary company Dürkopp Fördertechnik GmbH (a leading provider of conveyer technology) to Knapp AG, an Austrian company, for 10 million euros.

The management of DA further announced that temporary staffing, which had permeated almost all functions since February 2009 (averaging as much as 40% of the workforce) was to continue until the crisis was over. Senior employees were urged to take early retirement. Material costs were further reduced by a wide margin in the second half of the year. In addition, the trouser sewing machine specialist, Beisler GmbH was relocated from Hösbach to Bielefeld. Getting out of crisis took more than cost cutting obviously. In exploring growth avenues, Heer made it clear that DA intended to expand the business in China and would increase investment in sales and marketing activities there.

To everyone's great relief, the situation started to turn for the better in the first quarter of 2010, which saw sales jump nearly 40%. Learning from the struggles of the pervious couple of years, DA's management realized that the company needed to become more resilient and search for new growth drivers. One promising field was the industrial sector, selling machines to the automotive industry and producers of upholstery and technical textiles. DA, endowed with its technological capital, was well positioned to assume a leading spot in this sector.

Meanwhile, DA's parent company, the SGSB Group, was undergoing a great deal of turmoil. As China was not immune to the global financial crisis, SGSB's sewing machine business there also suffered from a severe sales meltdown. Staff at all hierarchical levels saw their salaries and benefits trimmed and a series of cost-saving measures was introduced. On March 24, 2010, partially under the influence of its then major shareholder, Pudong New Area State-owned Assets Supervision and Administration Commission, the SGSB Group entered into a framework agreement on strategic cooperation with Zoje Sewing Machine Co., Ltd., one of the leading private sewing machine companies in China.

Pertaining to the agreement, ShangGong Europe transferred 2.378 million shares, equivalent to 29% of its stake in DA, to Zoje Europe GmbH, a wholly owned subsidiary of Zoje, which became DA's second-largest shareholder. In this transaction, the total value of the shares was reckoned at 8.63 million euros, or 3.63 euros per share. Rumor had it that according to the original arrangement, Zoje was supposed to take over a larger share of DA at a later point of time, although SGSB would have remained the absolute major shareholder. In the end, the initial plan was not executed due to changes at both companies. Nevertheless, the paths of these two Chinese sewing machinery heavyweights would cross again several years later, when they competed for the acquisition of another German sewing machine manufacturer.

As the Chinese proverb goes, "a crisis is an opportunity riding the dangerous wind." Amid the financial crisis, demand from the automotive industry in Asia, particularly in China, remained resilient and was forecast to boom for years to come. Betting that it would be the next blue ocean for industrial sewing, the SGSB Group spared no effort to support DA in its development of machines for automotive clients. The central pillar of DA's development endeavor was improving upon the

M-type series, which was used as the basis for medium- to heavy-duty sewing machines, debuting as early as 2002. Since then, the M-type has become synonymous with top-quality industrial sewing equipment. With SGSB's backing, DA was able to continue to advance the M-type series at a time when the sewing machine industry as a whole was going through its most difficult period. Major improvement was made by drastically reducing the number of parts used, which resulted in a considerable reduction in complexity-related costs. This change allowed customers to further optimize their assembly processes and significantly reduce lead time. The M-type turned out to be instrumental in pulling the company out of the crisis and securing key accounts from the automotive and upholstery industries.

Under Heer's leadership, DA recovered and posted double-digit revenue growth back-to-back in 2010 and 2011, topping operative earnings before the crisis. Thanks to innovation and cost-saving measures, its EBIT margin improved by almost 2% points to 9.5% in 2011. Despite the successful turnaround, Heer's second honeymoon with SGSB was too short-lived. He credited the recovery largely to the launch of new products, particularly the M-type series, which was very popular across the Atlantic in high-end medium- to heavy-duty segment. When setting the directions for the future, Heer insisted that DA should allocate more resources to this area, and eventually focus solely on this segment going forward. While acknowledging the relevance of the medium- to heavy-duty segment, the Chinese shareholder favored a more balanced approach, citing the untapped potential in the traditional clothing industry in less developed countries in particular. Based out of China, SGSB's leadership noted a clear trend toward automation and optimization of sewing processes in the clothing industry. This trend emerged in the wake of continuous wage increases, as China's demographic dividend was diminishing. SGSB and DA were presented with a precious window of opportunity to crack the Chinese market. As the market demanded higher-value products, DA with its technological know-how should have been better poised to profit from the market transition than it was 10 years ago. After rounds of consultation, it was not possible to reconcile the divergent views within the management as to the best growth strategy for DA. Consequently, Heer stepped down from the management board after two and half years' tenure.

In 2012, Dietrich Eickhoff, a DA veteran and a local Bielefelder, was appointed the new spokesperson of the management board. Eickhoff had started his career in the 1970s as a trainee at Dürkoppwerke, the predecessor of Dürkopp Adler. He had a strong sales and technical background, which was conducive to a customer-oriented growth strategy and further expansion in international markets, especially in China. As he had also been a member of the DA team that had conducted the initial negotiations with ShangGong back in 2004, he was already very familiar with the modus operandi of the SGSB leadership and had a common understanding with them. The continuity within the senior management team meant there was no need for a realignment on the strategic orientation of DA and SGSB. It was agreed that, in Bielefeld, DA would focus on high-end equipment, while SGSB in Shanghai would mainly serve the mass market with economy products.

2012 was a satisfying year, as sales grew by 8% year on year. Its unique technological advantage enabled DA to continuously increase its profitability, unlike many of its competitors. Its operative profit margin in 2012 exceeded 15% for the first time in at least a decade. However, the picture behind this success was mixed: the core markets in Europe, which represented the lion's share of DA's revenue, remained challenging due to stagnant demand, while the emerging economies in Asia grew increasingly important as economic growth there continued. In China specifically, there were strong signs that the market was maturing as the labor costs rocketed and clothing manufacturers, among other industries, were gradually moving their production sites to lower-cost neighboring countries, such as Vietnam and Bangladesh. Given that automated, higher-end machines were expected to be in demand in China, DA hoped to win new customers that were willing to pay for premium products.

5.3.3 Phase 3 (2013–2016): New Horizons—DA Steers Toward the World Leadership

From 2013 onwards, SGSB went on offensive again. In a short period of time, it acquired two firms and obtained a minority interest in a third. All of the firms were from Germany's *Mittelstand* (medium-sized companies) with advanced technology in their respective fields and sound reputations. ShangGong Europe, which for a long time had only consisted of DA as its sole investment, now set out to take on greater operative responsibility in steering its portfolio companies.

5.3.3.1 Pfaff Industriesysteme und Maschinen AG

On March 28, 2013, a long-anticipated strategic move materialized. ShangGong (Europe) Holding Corp. GmbH, acquired 100% of Pfaff Industriesysteme und Maschinen AG in Kaiserslautern. Pfaff has had a turbulent history, full of ups and downs for over a century, as was recounted in a documentary film released in 2014. The renowned manufacturer, founded in 1862, used to be Europe's biggest sewing machine company. In the early days, Pfaff produced domestic sewing machines exclusively. It was not until 1908 that Pfaff brought the first industrial sewing machines to the market, making a distinction between domestic and industrial sewing machines for the first time in history. Pfaff Industrial quickly became a highly esteemed quality brand in the sewing trade. In 1960, the company was listed on the Frankfurt Stock Exchange. In the1980s, Pfaff suffered a serious downturn in its major customers from the shoe and clothes-making industries. Adverse market situation coupled with a number of managerial mistakes heralded decades of turmoil ahead. Pfaff was changed hands multiple times and even filed for bankruptcy twice, in 1999 and 2008, respectively. Nevertheless, Pfaff maintained its prominence in various sewing and welding technologies. It was particularly strong in automatic sewing units, medium–heavy duty sewing machines, and welding machines.

At the turn of the twenty-first century, the center of gravity of the global textile industry accelerated drifting to Asia. Pfaff followed the trend, establishing a joint venture with its Chinese partner Zoje Sewing Machine Co., Ltd. Pfaff subsequently managed to open its own plant in Taicang, near Shanghai, and took over all the shares in the joint venture from Zoje. The 100% owned company was a main pillar of production and market strategy for the Pfaff Group and was deemed the future centerpiece of its China activities. In 2008, around 20,000 Pfaff industrial sewing machines and related controls and drives were manufactured at the Taicang plant.

In 2009, following a period of insolvency for Pfaff, Joachim Richter, the owner of a medium-sized German manufacturing company, was successful in his bid to take over the company. Although both the works unions and local politicians had rooted for Richter, his restructuring plan did not pan out well. The company continued to lose market share and make losses. In August 2012, Richter conceded and handed over his entire stake in Pfaff to a trustee. By the end of 2012, Pfaff's total assets were worth 20 million euros, while liabilities exceeded 26 million euros. The company was practically insolvent after making seven-digit losses for several years in a row.

SGSB was determined to acquire Pfaff this time and gained the upper hand over its competitors, including Zoje. Although there had been a joint venture between Zoje and Pfaff, and Zoje was even a minority shareholder in DA, it was SGSB's proven track record with DA that convinced all the stakeholders. Zhang, chairman and CEO of SGSB, personally led the deal negotiations, which was considered a key success factor in closing the deal. SGSB took over all equity in Pfaff for a symbolic one euro. In accordance with the acquisition agreement, SGSB injected 24.1 million euros, of which 4.8 million was paid-in capital, 11.5 million was shareholder debt, and 7.8 million was to expand operations in China and Southeast Asia. Following its lost bid, Zoje sold the entirety of its shares in DA back to SGSB for 13.9 million euros in late 2014, reaping over 60% return on the investment.

Pfaff and DA, two German giants in industrial sewing machines, went back over 150 years in head-to-head competition. Upon completion of the transaction, the two archenemies joined forces under the umbrella of ShangGong Europe. Cornelia Mast, acting spokesperson of the management board at Pfaff remained in office after the acquisition and was responsible for finance, administration, and HR. In addition, SGSB appointed two other board members, Wang Qing, previously deputy general manager of ShangGong Europe, and Friedbert Schulz, a sales and marketing executive who worked for Pfaff from 1972 to 1999 before joining DA.

Through ShangGong Europe, SGSB indirectly set the strategic directions of the two subsidiary companies, although they operated independently. Nevertheless, it was clear to all stakeholders that Pfaff's business activities had to be coordinated with those of DA and SGSB, otherwise it would not be possible to bring Pfaff back to profitability.

The synergy between the two companies became already evident in 2014, only 1 year after the deal was closed. Pfaff turned a profit again—the first time in 12 years—and DA continually improved both its top and bottom lines. Sales jumped 15% in 2014, while operating margin rose by an impressive 5% points. This strong growth trend and healthy margin has been maintained to date (Fig. 5.4).

The success achieved in this short timeframe was the product of a plethora of optimization measures. There was low-hanging fruit as the longtime competitors could finally stop underbidding each other on tenders. This had a sizable impact on both their top and bottom lines. On the production side, similar to the changes implemented at DA previously, the manufacturing division was optimized and some processes were outsourced to locations abroad, such as in the Czech Republic and

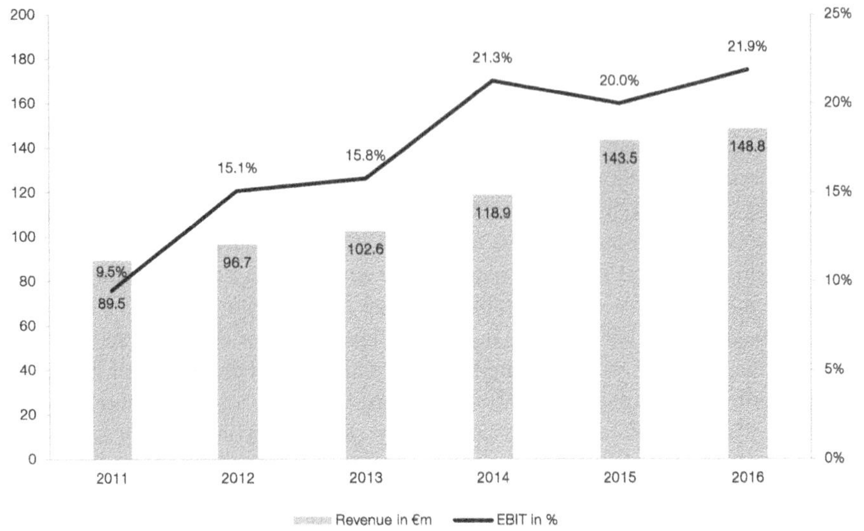

Fig. 5.4 DA's sales and operating margin (2011–2016). Source: ShangGong Europe

China, utilizing comparable cost advantages. Further potential was seized in R&D, procurement, and particularly in sales and marketing activities.

In an interview in 2016, the deputy chairman of the works council at Pfaff, Wolfgang Biffar, commented on the takeover: "I see it as overwhelmingly positive." He admired the reliability of the new owner despite all cultural differences: "Commitments have always been respected. For 2 years, there has been a steady increase in jobs in Kaiserslautern. Now we have 218 employees," he said.

5.3.3.2 KSL Keilmann Group

On July 31, 2013, just a few months after acquiring Pfaff, SGSB bought all shares in the family-run business KSL Keilmann Group from its sole owner Robert Keilmann for 18.5 million euros. At the time of the transaction, the KSL Keilmann Group employed about 100 people and had distribution partners around the world. The group consisted of three companies: KSL Keilmann Sondermaschinenbau GmbH (KSL), a producer of special machines for processing all types of technical textiles, including fiber composites; KSA GmbH & Co. KG (KSA), a producer of sewing technology with a focus on mattress manufacturing; and KSE GmbH, which acted solely as a sales organization for KSL, particularly in overseas markets, such as Asia and North America. Werner Keilmann, Robert Keilmann's father, founded the group in 1964 in Lorsch, 60 km south of Frankfurt am Main.

KSL, the most valuable of all three Keilmann sibling companies, offered a wide range of products, including CNC machines, multi-needle sewing machines, robotic systems, gluing and welding units, and automatic production lines. Its innovative 3D robot sewing units were unparalleled technologically and could be programmed to perform complex sewing and welding jobs (see Fig. 5.5 for impression of KSL's

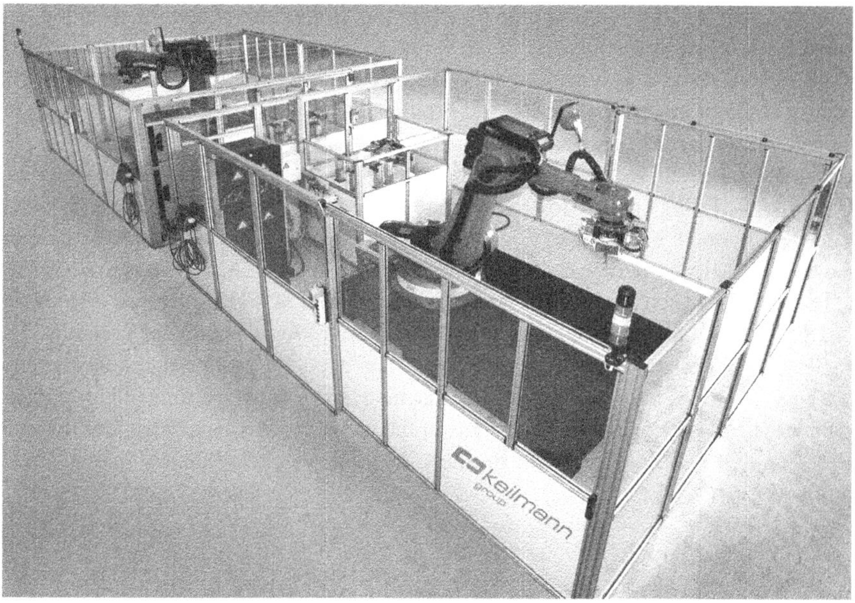

Fig. 5.5 KSL basic 3D-robot sewing unit KL 500. Source: ShangGong Europe

robot sewing unit). It found its customer base in new segments with great growth potential, such as aerospace, automotive, and environmental protection industries.

In order to better exploit the synergy, KSL was merged into Pfaff in March 2015, while keeping the KSL brand alive. The production sites in Lorsch and Kaiserslautern remained in operation after the merger but the production of mattress systems was relocated from the site in Altenburg to Kaiserslautern. High-tech equipment and customized machines were developed, designed, and made in Lorsch under the KSL label. The new Pfaff was led by an experienced management board consisting of Cornelia Mast, Robert Keilmann, and Chen Yongwu. Chen used to work for Zoje, Pfaff's former joint venture partner. Thanks to the experience gained from DA, the integration of Pfaff and KSL went smoothly. By the end of 2016, the financial results of both companies had improved remarkably.

SGSB's shopping spree continued in 2016, when Zhang had been widely recognized as a successful investor in the sewing industry. This time, however, SGSB decided to look beyond sewing machines. In mid-January 2016, after months of negotiation, ShangGong Europe acquired 26% equity in H. Stoll AG und Co. KG in Reutlingen for 28.5 million euros, becoming the single largest shareholder. The remainder of the shares were scattered among the 12 members of the founding family.

The family-run company boasted a long history, just like DA and Pfaff. Founded in 1873, it was one of the largest and most innovative manufacturers of automatic flat knitting machines in the world. Under pressure from the ever increasing competition in the global sewing and knitting equipment market, the shareholders began actively looking for potential investors 5 years ago. SGSB fitted the bill as the perfect investor, as it had been in the same playfield for a long time, it had the capital much needed for future investment, and more importantly, had a proved track record of working with German hidden champions in a responsible and sustainable way. The acquisition of a minority stake in Stoll brought about a reshuffle within the management structure of SGSB's European operations.

On March 15, 2016, Mast, a former executive at Pfaff, moved to Stoll as the new CFO after fulfilling her mission to integrate the once insolvent Pfaff into ShangGong Europe. Robert Keilmann resigned as spokesperson of Pfaff's management board on August 31, 2016 for personal reasons. He was succeeded by Alfred Wadle, a returnee to Pfaff, who had served as the second CEO of DA after SGSB took it over. From then on, the Pfaff management board consisted of Alfred Wadle and Chen Yongwu.

With Stoll on board, SGSB was stronger than ever and well prepared for the next big goal: world leadership of the sewing machine business. At the time of writing, two Japanese firms occupy the top two spots in the industry in terms of revenue, Juki and Brothers. SGSB is not far behind Brothers in revenue and it is already market leader profit-wise.

5.4 Growth Initiatives

DA has been transformed from the troubled child of a large conglomerate family to the poster child of SGSB's overseas operations. Under the umbrella of SGSB, DA has not only maintained its innovation capabilities, it also has caught up on production efficiency and the exploitation of new markets. Over the years, DA has grown revenue sustainably while improving its profit margins. Its stock price has risen from 2.3 euros 12 years ago to near 36 euros in 2016, and it has continued its growth momentum in 2017 (see Fig. 5.6).

Joined by Pfaff, KSL, and Stoll in the brand portfolio, DA was well prepared to conquer the next frontier. It was also time to part ways with ShangGong Europe. The latter had been established to serve as an investment vehicle for SGSB in Europe. For a long time, DA was the only business administered by ShangGong Europe, both of which were essentially led by the same management team.

Zhang, chairman and CEO of SGSB, envisioned something bigger for ShangGong Europe, namely, that it should become the driving force behind SGSB's sewing machine business worldwide, coordinating and steering brand strategy, marketing, sales, procurement, production, and R&D.

To institutionalize the transformation, Eickhoff was invited to resign as the spokesperson of DA's management board in March 2016 so as to concentrate on ShangGong Europe's future operations. His position at DA was assumed by Michael Kilian, who was previously in charge of quality and developing control technology. To ensure the continuity of DA's strategic orientation, Eickhoff stayed with DA as a member of the supervisory board. In the meantime, Zheng Ying, the long-term chief representative of the major shareholder, kept her dual executive responsibilities at both DA and the holding company.

Fig. 5.6 DA share price development (2005–2017). Source: Dürkopp Adler

The management team of the new ShangGong Europe had one clear mandate: profitable growth. ShangGong now aims to become number one in the world for textile manufacturing technologies within the next 5 years. In addition to striving for growth, it should also achieve better margins than the competition. ShangGong is already very close to the Japanese firm Brothers, which currently holds the number two spot globally, while the world champion, Juki, has about three times ShangGong's revenue.

A ShangGong Europe growth strategy for the next 5 years was articulated in a strategy document in September 2016. The success of the growth strategy rests on three pillars: continuous innovation; market penetration in Asia, especially in China; and further M&A's followed by brand integration and coordination.

5.4.1 Continuous Innovation

SGSB leadership had always attached great importance to R&D and supported innovation in words and actions. DA, and latterly Pfaff and KSL, have been able to rely on financial aid from their major shareholder, allowing them to continuously invest in new product development and earning them various awards for innovations as a result. For example, DA was honored with a Texprocess Innovation Award in 2013 for developing a new automatic sleeve setting sewing machine and PFAFF Industrial received the same award for its "Smart Seaming Sewing Control 2.0". Also that year, KSL developed the world's first robotic sewing units for aviation and wind energy applications.

Thanks to its firm grasp of market trends and the strategic directions of the major shareholder, DA had a head start in advancing its product portfolio. When other companies were competing over stand-alone machines, i.e. one machine operated by one person, DA had already begun developing special automated machines pre-programmed with every single step in the production process, improving efficiency and accuracy significantly. In addition to whole products, DA also actively promoted the development of new electronic control units and pioneered machine-to-machine (M2M) systems, pioneering the application of Industry 4.0 to keep abreast of ever-changing customer needs. With the integration of KSL, SGSB will be able to make progress in cutting-edge technologies, such as robotic cutting, composed connection, and carbon fiber sewing. The future product portfolio at ShangGong Europe will not only focus on mechanical engineering but also increasingly on software engineering with the advancement of Industry 4.0 technology. In short, the innovation efforts at ShangGong Europe will focus on three areas: machines, smart manufacturing/automation, and value-adding services based on big data (see Fig. 5.7).

5.4.2 Market Penetration in Asia

The second pillar of the growth strategy is expansion into new Asian markets. Eickhoff reflected on DA's global strategy and the development of the global sewing machine market: "The market trend changed 10 years ago to our detriment, but it is now changing again, and this time to our advantage." He was referring to the fact that due to the upgrade of manufacturing in China and elsewhere, there is an increased need for sewing machines with a higher degree of automation, a strong suit of DA. Nevertheless, DA learned a hard lesson that it will not work to simply copy European technology and make stripped-down versions of it. The last few years have not seen a major uplift in orders from China or the rest of Asia (see Fig. 5.8).

There are many reasons why a European sewing machine company would fail in China. To start with, customer needs are different in the European and Chinese markets, and European manufacturers often underestimate the magnitude of these differences. In DA's case, it is used to European customers that typically produce high-value items in high volume, and relatively speaking, are less concerned with lead time. In contrast, the large Chinese manufacturers usually make clothing for multiple brands and need to change style sets frequently, sometimes up to three times a day. This requires a quick turnaround of application engineering from the sewing machine provider. In addition, the raw materials required, such as textiles and threads, can vary widely depending on the specific region, therefore flexible configuration is quintessential for the machines. In order to be successful in the China market, SGSB's German brands have to be more agile and more responsive to market requirements. The localization of R&D and application engineering will be mandatory. For the last few years, China has mainly served as a procurement and production center for ShangGong Europe. Going forward, cooperation on new product development will have to be strengthened in order for the company to be competitive in China. The economy segment is still the largest segment in the

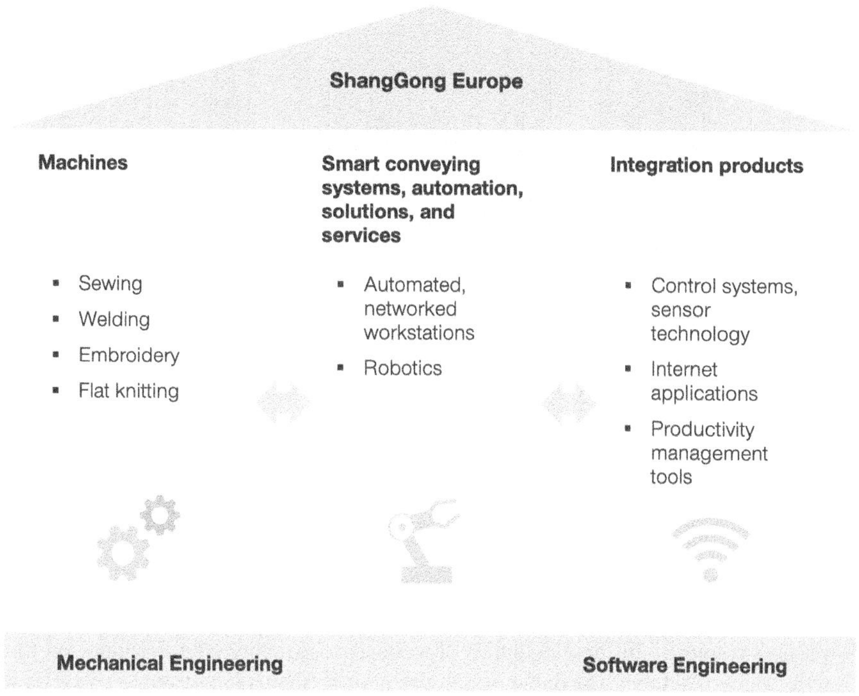

Fig. 5.7 ShangGong Europe's future product range. Source: ShangGong Europe

country with approximately 1.5 million units sold in 2016, but it is a tough market. Juki, the leading Japanese brand used to have 50% of the market back in 2000. Its share has halved since then and Chinese players now dominate. SGSB's local brand SG Gemsy has about a 10% market share, while four or five leading Chinese sewing machine companies control about a 60% market share collectively. As the German brands are associated with high-end, expensive products, management is considering exploring market opportunities in the mid-range segment with a new product line with less features and more competitive prices. Such products will also be more suitable for the other Asian markets. Plans include introducing *Pfaff Industrial Traditional*, a sub-brand of Pfaff to cater to this segment. The sub-brand's products will be produced entirely in China.

There are other promising signs on the horizon. The newest subsidiary company, KSL, has already secured small-scale but highly profitable business with its first customers for sewing robots in China through SGSB's local network that includes Hongdu Air, COMAC, Hafei, and Beijing Aerospace Institute, just to name a few.

ShangGong Europe is charged with spearheading growth in international markets. The focus in the years to come is clearly on expanding its sales and marketing reach in Southeast Asia. New sales subsidiaries are planned in India and Bangladesh to be in the vicinity of the rapidly growing opportunities in the region as the industrial sewing machine market in China is currently in flux with production sites being relocated to

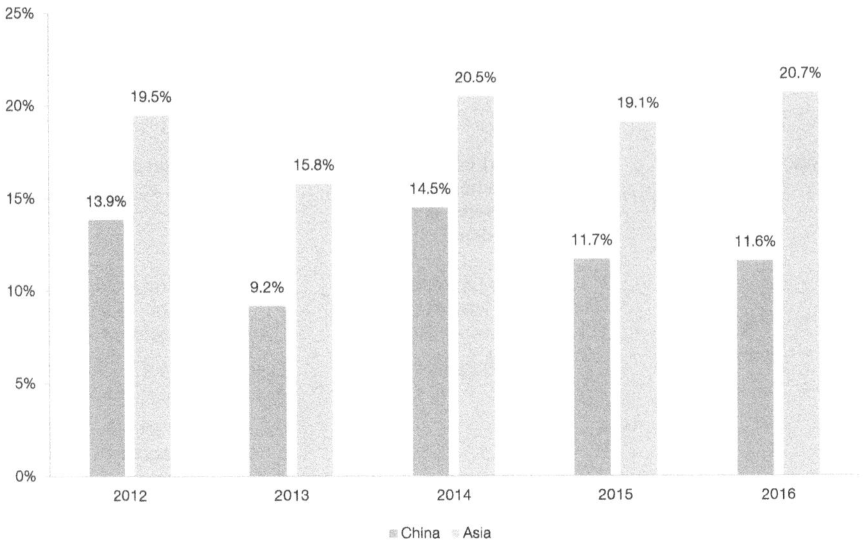

Fig. 5.8 DA's revenue share in China and Asia. Source: ShangGong Europe

lower-cost countries. In these countries, lower-end commodity-type machines prevail, exactly where China was a couple of decades ago. If ShangGong Europe succeeds in scaling up business over there, the SGSB Group will be better able to utilize its production capacity in China while maintaining a healthy margin. However, challenges lie in finding the right channel mix, and above all, the right brand mix.

5.4.3 Brand Integration and Coordination

Through a series of acquisitions, SGSB has built up a rich brand portfolio (see Fig. 5.9). Besides the well-known names Dürkopp Adler, Pfaff Industrial, and KSL, SGSB owns two niche German brands. One is Beisler, specializing in premium sewing automation solutions for men's trousers; the other is Mauser, a traditional brand for sewing machines with a variety of applications. On its home turf in China, SBSG has SG Gemsy, making industrial sewing machines and providing automation solutions for a wide range of applications. As SGSB and ShangGong Europe expand further, the brand portfolio is expected to grow even larger.

Since the acquisition of Pfaff and KSL, integration has focused on the housekeeping side, i.e. procurement, production, and product development. In order to unlock various brands' potential, the topic of front-end synergy still has to be properly addressed. This means the brands need to act in concert over sales and marketing, with clearly defined segments and value propositions for each brand. Internal discussions about synergies have been conducted between group headquarters and all subsidiary companies. High-level brand segmentation has been documented in the 5-year growth strategy plan mentioned above. In essence, the objective is to minimize overlap and assign the brands

Fig. 5.9 SGSB's major industrial sewing machine brands. Source: SGSB Group

to specific customer segments where they can secure relative competitive edges. In the meantime, the brands will be grouped into premium and commodity clusters, each of which will have shared sales and marketing functions. In the next few years, it will remain a challenging task for ShangGong Europe and the SGSB Group to articulate and operationalize the brand strategy, especially when it comes to new products and/or regions. ShangGong Europe will play a pivotal role in integrating the brands. It will be more hands-on with the sales and marketing functions of all brands in addition to production and R&D. ShangGong Europe will also coordinate the go-to-market strategy for new sales regions.

When asked about his personal vision for SGSB, Zhang said that SGSB would concentrate on a number of areas in particular:

- **Sewing technology for new materials, above all carbon fiber:** This material has broad applications due to its strength, rigidity, and light weight
- **Automated joining or cutting equipment:** In Zhang's view, sewing is fundamentally about joining two materials together. Therefore, knitting, welding, gluing, and fiber placement are all closely related to sewing, while cutting is an interesting area to be explored, being the flip side of joining. Both joining and cutting have great potential as they can be applied to a broad range of areas for the same type of customers
- **New and emerging industries, such as aerospace and the defense industry:** In the next decade, the aircraft industry is expected to boom in China, stimulating demand for new downstream applications

SGSB is keen to gain a foothold in new business areas. However, this goal hides Zhang's greater ambition. "The size of the global industrial sewing machine market is limited. There is a ceiling for growth in sight for SGSB. We need to look further afield and find a new business area that can take SGSB to the next level." This attitude gives hints why SGSB has come so far in only 12 years, from a time when the company faced bankruptcy and risked being torn apart.

5.5 Closing Remarks

Thanks to DA's stellar performance, SGSB and Zhang have been in the spotlight for a while. It was a trailblazer and a benchmark in the recent history of Chinese direct investment in Germany. What makes SGSB stand out is its commitment to its German subsidiary companies. It has been proved time and again over the last 12 years that the combination of a German company with a Chinese investor works.

A serial investor or industrial entrepreneur?

Zhang has frequently been championed by the media as a successful serial investor. He himself seemed to identify with an industrial entrepreneur with great vision. Investors inject capital, entrepreneurs instill a common vision. We had the opportunity to ask him personally what we feel is the most pertinent question: How was DA able to make such a turnaround with a Chinese owner when the German owner failed?

A clear strategy based on astutely judging market trends and building mutual trust with the management.

According to Zhang, DA was a hidden gem. Its technology was world-class, as ShangGong was lagging at least 30 years behind. DA was very much a technologically driven company, like many German companies still are. However, it overslept as the global textile industry drifted to the East. SGSB valued DA's technology and developed it further, while also transforming DA into a more market-driven company and implementing efficiency-enhancing measures. Shareholder value increased mainly due to the integration being so carefully managed.

Even Mr. Zhang's verbal promises are always kept
—Dietrich Eickhoff, managing director of ShangGong Europe

Actions speak louder than words. In the beginning, the employees were obviously skeptical about the Chinese. However, over time, the Chinese owner won not only their trust but also their respect, particularly after the 2008–2009 financial crisis. DA used to be a tiny piece of the FAG/Schaeffler industrial conglomerate with shareholders that did not care about its fortune. It is a completely different story with SGSB. DA is highly valued and plays a vital role in leading the growth of the SGSB Group as a whole.

Being a traditional state-owned enterprise, SGSB has emerged as an internationalized group with 15 out of its 30 subsidiaries located abroad. Half of the 4600-strong workforce is non-Chinese. ShangGong Europe generates about 70% of SGSB's sewing machine business today and this figure is growing. Soon it should be probably be renamed "ShangGong Overseas", as its operations extend to markets beyond Europe.

At the Texprocess 2017 in Frankfurt, DA won the prestigious Innovation Award with its newly minted Qondac 4.0 network solution, which enables real-time production optimization, supports individualization, and reduces cost by remotely maintaining networks of up to 1500 sewing machines.

2017 heralded the next stage of development for SGSB. At the time of writing, the SGSB Group has completed an initial program of corporate restructuring as part of a reform pilot project initiated by governmental authorities. At the end of the restructuring period, the agency dilemma will be largely dissolved and the leadership will have greater responsibility and will be more able to fuel future growth. Twelve years ago, SGSB headed for the West. Now it is turning back toward the East for its next 12-year cycle of Odyssey.

6 Joyson Electronics/Preh: Be Part of Something Big

This case study was published with kind permission of the Joyson Group.

Like many privately owned companies in the Yangtze River Delta, Joyson Electronics came from humble beginnings just little over a decade ago. It began its adventure overseas in 2011 by acquiring the German firm Preh GmbH, a bold move which the media described as "snake swallowing elephant". In the following years, the additions of QUIN GmbH, IMA automation, TechniSat Digital GmbH's automotive division and Key Safety Systems Inc. (a U.S.-based firm), enriched Joyson Electronics' up- and down-stream industrial chains and expanded its business boundaries. Back in 2006, 2 years after its inception, Joyson Electronics only generated 20 million yuan in revenue. The next 10 years saw explosive growth, as the revenue had risen to 18.6 billion yuan (or 23.9 billion yuan if the full-year revenues of KSS and TechniSat were consolidated), almost 1000 times higher. Some may attribute all this to good fortune. While luck played its part, what were the other factors that lay behind this success story? How did cross-border M&A's help regenerate Joyson Electronics?

In the wake of the Reform and Opening-up Policy of the 1980s, large numbers of family-owned companies came into existence, remarkably concentrated in the provinces such as Zhejiang and Jiangsu on China's east coast. After the first few years of rapid development, the economic downturn hit these privately-owned enterprises especially hard. Wang Jianfeng, who also goes by Jeff Wang, came from such a family that had founded a company before the downturn. When he took over his family's business, Ningbo Yongxing Vehicle Accessories, in 1993, it was undergoing grave financial difficulties. To get out of the adverse situation, Wang expanded the business to interior accessories from its origins producing fasteners for cars. In 1999, the company turned around and generated revenue of several million yuan. In the same year, the US automotive supplier powerhouse TRW Automotive began gearing up its fastener business after 5 years of exploration on its own in the Chinese market and was looking for an appropriate Chinese partner to set up a joint venture with. Wang sold the majority of shares in his firm to TRW Automotive, which

J. Y. Yang et al., *Chinese M&As in Germany*, Management for Professionals,
https://doi.org/10.1007/978-3-319-99405-5_6

then formed TRW Ningbo Components & Fastening Systems Co., Ltd. Wang became general manager at the new company and later assumed the role of general manager of strategy development at TRW China.

After 5 years at TRW China, Wang decided to move on and start over with his own venture in 2004. According to the vice president of Joyson Holding, Guo Zhiming, it was the experience at TRW that helped Wang come to realize the potential of the automotive electronics segment. "He was a young man in his twenties, when he sold most of the shares in his family business and joined a prestigious automotive supplier as the general manager of its China business. It was quite an experience. Not only did this deepen his understanding of the global auto market, the knowledge he acquired later also assisted his company in its overseas expansion, because Jeff had lived the equity change of his family business himself and understood how to carry out value-adding integration and how to motivate the management of the acquired company and maximize the synergy."

From the very beginning, the firm made understanding customer demands a top priority and then incorporated these insights into its R&D, design processes, and production. "Other firms started out by copying existing products, we began with R&D," said the company's co-founder, President and Vice CEO Fan Jinhong. Such strategy slowed down Joyson Electronics' revenue growth initially, which amounted to 20 million yuan after the first 2 years. However, the R&D-based strategy paid off in the long run and laid a solid foundation for its future endeavors.

Joyson Electronics first caught public attention in 2010 when it conducted a series of overseas M&A's and became active in the capital market:

- **A-share listing:** In 2010, Joyson Electronics was listed on the stock exchange through a reverse merger of Liaoyuan Deheng Co., Ltd. One year later, Joyson Electronics started restructuring and injected new assets into the public company upon approval from the China Securities Regulatory Commission. The company became an A-share listed company on the Shanghai Stock Exchange, which is great achievement for a private enterprise
- **First M&A abroad:** In 2011, Joyson Electronics acquired 74.9% of shares in Preh GmbH, a German automotive electronics supplier with a long history. In December 2012, Joyson Electronics acquired the rest of the shares and became the sole owner of the company. It then injected the assets of Preh GmbH into the listed company and became the first automotive electronics company on the Shanghai Stock Exchange with an international brand
- **Serial overseas M&A's:** In 2013, Joyson Electronics acquired IMA Automation through Preh GmbH, followed by the acquisition of QUIN, a manufacturer of high-end interior accessories and steering wheels, in 2014. In 2016, Joyson Electronics became the 100% shareholder of EVANA Automation through Preh IMA (PIA). In the same year, it took over KSS, a leading manufacturer of auto safety systems based in the US, and TechniSat Automotive from Germany, for more than 1.1 billion dollars

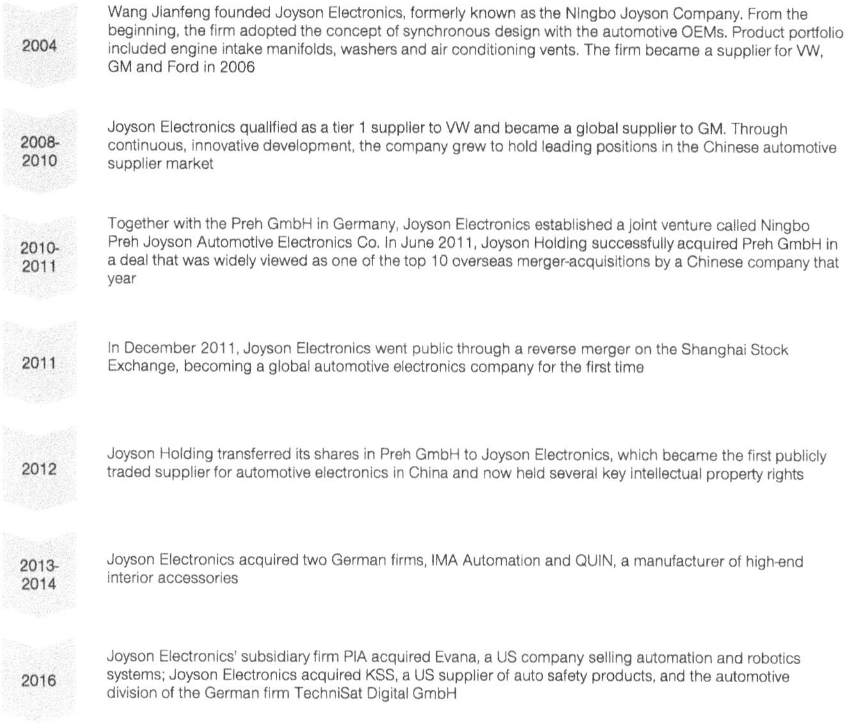

Fig. 6.1 Milestones of Joyson Electronics' development (2004–2016). Source: Joyson Electronics

Through the actions above, Joyson Electronics, previously a small company with an annual revenue of 20 million yuan, rocketed up to become a role model for the auto electronics and smart manufacturing industry in China, generating sales revenue of nearly 20 billion yuan in 2016. See the milestones of Joyson Electronics as follows (Fig. 6.1).

The array of overseas M&A's boosted Joyson Electronics' revenue almost a thousand times in 10 years (see Fig. 6.2). Following the successful integration of Preh GmbH, Joyson Electronics continued its expansion for the years to come, acquiring the German firms IMA Automation, QUIN, and TechniSat Automotive, and the US firms KSS and EVANA. Successive M&A's have been the primary driver through which Joyson Electronics has internationalized itself, restructured, and upgraded its technology.

More importantly, with the help of the acquired companies, Joyson Electronics expanded its business portfolio worldwide and enriched its upstream and downstream industrial chains, bringing forward all business lines at the same time (see Fig. 6.3).

Starting out as a challenger, Joyson Electronics embarked on the journey to be become a heavy-weight automotive supplier with forecast sales of more than 30 billion yuan for 2017. Joyson Electronics is a classic example of a company

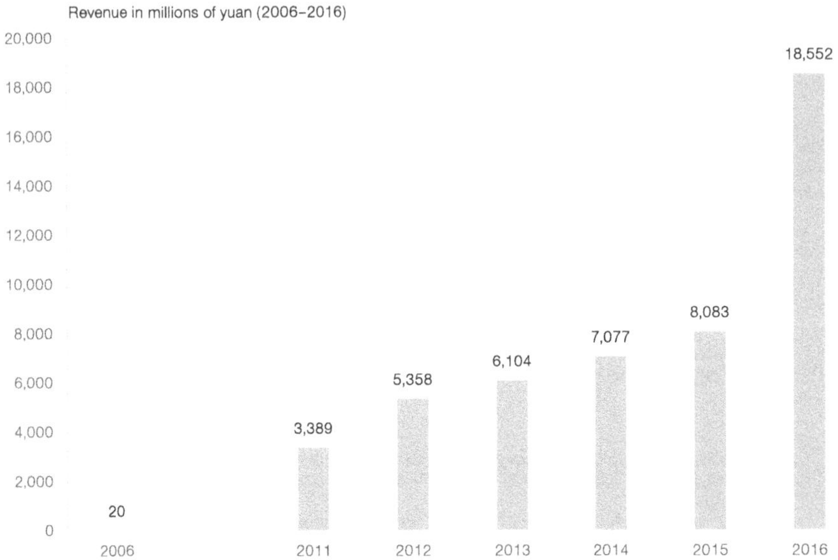

Fig. 6.2 Revenue of Joyson Electronics (2006–2016). Source: Joyson Electronics

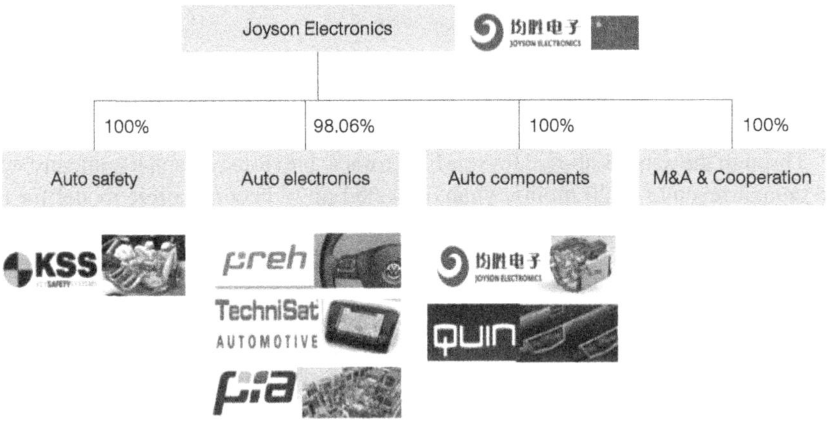

Fig. 6.3 Joyson Electronics' business units (2016). Source: Joyson Electronics

that has expanded through a combination of organic growth and M&A's. The deal between Joyson Electronics and Preh was the catalyst for the accelerated growth. Acquiring Preh was not only a significant transaction in its own right, it was also the first important step in Joyson Electronics' global blueprint.

With revenue of just 1 billion yuan in 2010, Joyson Electronics spent a hefty 1.6 billion yuan on the acquisition of Preh, a firm with annual revenue of just shy of 400 million euros at the time. Four years later, Preh doubled the revenue to

800 million euros, realizing a compound annual growth rate of more than 20%. What made this acquisition so successful and how was the synergy effect tapped to the full?

6.1 Background

In its early days, Joyson Electronics produced functional parts and peripheral products for automotive OEM's. Early on, the management team declared the ambition to become a first-tier supplier. In 2006, Joyson Electronics set up a production site in Changchun to provide First Automotive Works with auto parts. Later, it managed to supply engine intake manifolds, washers, air conditioning vents etc. to leading car makers such as GM and Ford.

In 2004, when Joyson Holding was founded, there were only 2.4 million vehicles sold yearly in China. But since then, demand had picked up rapidly and the Chinese vehicle market had begun to overtake the developed economies, as the purchasing power of average households rose steadily. Today's global automotive industry is distinctly different from how it was before the 2008 financial crisis. When the Big Three US manufacturers (GM, Ford, and Chrysler) went through bankruptcy and subsequent restructuring, the gravity of the world automotive industry drifted toward China. In 2009, China became number one worldwide in terms of vehicle sales and has kept the leading position ever since (see Fig. 6.4).

On average, a passenger car consists of around 30,000 parts. Car makers rely heavily on a variety of suppliers to deliver the majority of the parts required to build a car. The dramatic increase in vehicle sales over the last decade in China has given

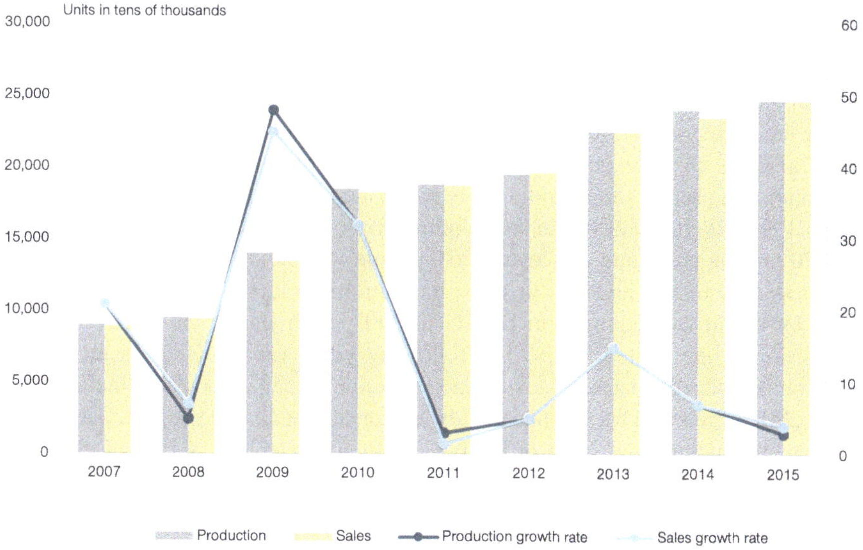

Fig. 6.4 Production and sales of motor vehicles in China (2007–2015). Source: China Association of Automobile Manufacturers

rise to numerous domestic automotive suppliers. Nevertheless, they are usually very weak in core technologies and innovation competence, compared to the world's leading companies.

In 2011, vehicle sales in China slowed down significantly, triggering a lot pressure on the car makers as well as the suppliers. There are two reasons for the fall in demand. On the one hand, the authorities withdrew consumer incentives to buy new cars and introduced restrictions on new car purchases in response to rising concerns about traffic congestion and air pollution in major cities. On the other, the automotive market entered a phase of consolidation after a decade of fast growth, which peaked in 2009 and 2010, as a significant proportion of pent-up demand had been fulfilled.

Although Joyson Electronics posted stable growth under these circumstances, it barely had any pricing power for lack of technological competence. The conundrum of demanding customers and aggressive competitors cut deeper into profit year over year. Recalling those old days, Jeff Wang, the chairman of Joyson Electronics, commented that "profit margin was as thin as a blade."

In response to customers' growing awareness about safety, comfort, and environmental protection, an increasing number of car makers have chosen to equip their medium to lower-class models with advanced electronic components, which used to be exclusive for the premium models. Consequently, the demand for electronic parts skyrocketed. After considerable research of market and industry trends, Joyson Electronics' management team came to the conclusion that automotive electronics should be the growth engine for the company in the future. It was during the search for a partner for the new venture that Preh came onto Joyson Electronics' radar.

Jakob Preh founded Preh GmbH in Bad Neustadt an der Saale, Germany, on March 11, 1919 to manufacture electronic components. With the advent of wireless radio technology, Jakob Preh invented the Preh Funk radio, first of its kind and a best-seller in Germany. From 1945 to 1988, Preh pioneered wireless radios and television parts and became market leader and standard setter at that time. By 1969, annual sales had hit a record 92 million German marks (or 47 million euros in today's currency). In 1988, the company branched out into automotive electronics with a range of new products, including air-conditioning control systems and potentiometric sensors for throttle valve position control.

In 1993, Rheinmetall Berlin AG acquired Preh GmbH, which achieved revenue of 220 million euros and employed 1970 people worldwide by the year 2000. The business now turned its focus to smart mechatronic solutions. Following the takeover by the private equity firm DBAG in 2003, Preh started the course of rapid expansion in the United States. The following years saw double-digit growth, as Preh built production sites in Mexico and Romania, among other places in the world.

In 2010, Preh ranked seventh worldwide for automotive electronics patents. Its 98 patents outnumbered some of the big automotive suppliers, such as Delphi and Continental. Preh also added battery management systems and driver control systems to its portfolio, which it supplied to premium car makers, including BMW, Mercedes-Benz, and Rolls-Royce. Despite its leading position in automotive electronics, Preh had a negligible operation in China, the largest motor vehicle market worldwide. It only supplied air-conditioning units to Shanghai Volkswagen at low volume and its presence in China was close to none, with only of a one-man office in Shanghai.

Since the beginning of 2006, the two joint ventures of Volkswagen Group in China, FAW-VW and Shanghai VW, had gradually adjusted their procurement strategies to increase share of local sourcing in China. Realizing it could be an excellent opportunity to expand business with Volkswagen, Joyson Electronics reached out to Preh in 2007 to discuss the possibility of setting up a joint venture to produce electronic parts for Volkswagen locally in China. Several senior managers of Joyson Electronics flew to Germany to persuade Preh to form a partnership. The mission failed, as the decision makers at Preh were not interested. However, there was a silver lining. From that, the management at Joyson Electronics and Preh GmbH kept dialogues and visited each other on a regular basis, building mutual understanding and trust.

The global financial crisis in 2008 handed Joyson Electronics a second chance, as DBAG looked to exit Preh GmbH. The European automotive industry was severely battered by the financial crisis, whereas China's automotive industry stayed resilient. Chinese investors soon came to the attention of DBAG. Intending to maintain Preh's existence as a going concern, DBAG defined a set of clear requirements for any potential bidder, namely, it should be a financially sound family-run business that could potentially be floated on the stock market. Being minority shareholders in the company, Preh's existing management also had considerable influence on picking the new owner.

Joyson Electronics invited Preh's management team to visit China. When they arrived, they were surprised to be taken to an undeveloped field where Wang Jianfeng announced the construction of an industrial park on the spot and told them about his grandiose business plan. The Germans reacted reticent. "They must have seen many pretentious Chinese businessmen. I'm sure they must have wondered if I was trying to trick them," shrugged Wang with a smile.

In 2009, the Preh management team learned that Joyson Electronics had acquired the automotive supplier Shanghai Huade, stepping up its game and emerging as a serious player in the field. The German managers decided they had to see this with their own eyes in China. Seeing that the greenfield industrial park was up and running and the businesses of Huade and Joyson Electronics were now unified, they were impressed by the Joyson Electronics' dedication to the automotive business and the speed at which it had followed through with its plans. This time, Joyson Electronics won the trust of the Preh managers.

As a result of what they had witnessed in China, Preh's management and the shareholders accepted the olive branch and entered into negotiation about a takeover. Although Joyson Electronics had experience working with foreign companies, none of its managers had relevant experience of overseas M&A's and this was a first for everyone on the Chinese side. They were not familiar with the M&A transaction procedure and the negotiation overran. Being determined not to miss out on valuable but transient market opportunities in China, Joyson Electronics found a joint venture with Preh GmbH in 2010 and started testing the waters as a team.

"The first months of the joint venture went by surprisingly well, instilling confidence in both parties to deepen the cooperation." recalled Guo. At that time,

Joyson Electronics was going through a lengthy approval process for public offering on the stock exchange. In order to conclude the acquisition of Preh, the Joyson management team decided that Joyson Holding would acquire Preh to begin with, and then inject Preh's assets into the to-be listed company (Joyson Electronics) by issuing new stock. On April 8, 2011, the shareholders of Joyson Holding and Preh GmbH signed the agreement and on June 27, 2011, the transaction was completed for a price of 1.6 billion yuan. All of Preh GmbH's technology patents were included in this deal.

Although M&A's by Chinese firms were nothing unusual by now, Joyson Electronics was the first to inject foreign assets to a listed company through the issuance of new stock. In mid-2011, Joyson Holding acquired approximately 74.9% of shares in Preh Holding, which held 94.1% of shares in Preh GmbH. In 2012, Joyson Electronics issued new stock to the majority shareholder Joyson Holdings and then it bought out the minority shareholders in Preh Holding, which owned 25.1% of the equity. In the meantime, Joyson Electronics also acquired 5.1% of shares in Preh GmbH from the remaining shareholders. At the end of the transactions, Preh went public in China indirectly.

6.2 Motivation and Strategy

"In 2010, group revenue from automotive parts surpassed 1.3 billion yuan. By 2011, this figure had risen to 2 billion yuan." said Joyson Holding's vice president, Guo. Although Joyson Electronics was a leading supplier of automotive parts and had invested tens of millions in R&D, a relatively large technological gap persisted between it and the leading global players. M&A's appeared to be an appealing thought to narrow the gap in a short timeframe.

An acquisition price of 1.6 billion yuan was nothing less than exorbitant for Joyson Electronics back then. With revenue of 1.3 billion yuan (approx. 144 million euros in 2010), Joyson Electronics could barely afford to buy the German firm, which made an annual revenue of 350 million euro at that time. So why dared Joyson make such big commitment to acquire Preh after all?

- **Hunger for better profitability:** Profit margin from functional parts was so low that Joyson Electronics had no choice but to explore alternative opportunities. "There were many private companies manufacturing plastic functional parts. If we had stuck with this business, we would have gotten lost in the competition and would not have made any profit. Fortune Global 500 companies like Siemens and Visteon dominated the high-end, high-profit business, which was extremely difficult to break into, due to the iron-clad specifications of the OEM's. We were unable to land any orders there, so it was imperative for us to make a breakthrough in technology. The fastest way to achieve so was to buy foreign companies with the advanced technology we need." said Wang.
- **Moving up the value chain:** The automotive electronics market is reckoned at many hundreds of billions of yuan. It was expected that Preh would not only complement

Joyson Holding's automotive parts portfolio, but would also help the company migrate up the value chain and expand overseas. Although the Chinese market for motor vehicles and automotive parts is enormous, local companies are weak in technology, particularly electronics, and core technologies remain privy to the foreign companies. "Without the acquisition, we would have needed a significant amount of time to be where we are now and had we attempted to do everything under our own steam, we would not be in the same league as the world's leading companies now," said Ye Shuping, vice president of Joyson Holding.

- **Resource complementarity:** Being in business in China for many years, Joyson Electronics had an astute sense of where the market would be headed for in the future, while Preh had exactly the type of the advanced technology Joyson Electronics needed. Moreover, Preh's activities in new markets, including China, were at a early stage, as its focus had been primarily on Europe and North America.
- **Access to key customers:** It was not possible for Joyson Electronics to gain access to international accounts on its own. In contrast, Preh had already established itself as a key supplier to leading automotive makers such as BMW for its signature iDrive system. Considering that the international car makers had been increasingly embracing a more flexible procurement strategy emphasizing local supplier partnerships in China, the combination of Joyson Electronics and Preh held bright future.
- **High intrinsic value:** Preh is a treasure in the automotive electronics sector. It succeeded in defending its standing throughout the European debt crisis and the subsequent global economic downturn. From 2005 to 2010, it achieved a compounded annual growth rate of 9.8%, which climbed again after the acquisition by Joyson Electronics, reaching 17.4%.
- **Common understanding:** Intercultural understanding was very important to both management teams. Through its interactions with Preh's management team over years, Joyson Electronics had built a good relationship with the German company as well as its then major shareholder, DBAG.

Regarding its strategy prior to the acquisition, Joyson Electronics' management team explains that the basic aim was for Preh to achieve double-digit growth worldwide, while the Chinese business would achieve revenue of a billion yuan within 5 years (i.e. by 2016). The German management team had thought it was not realistic at all, while the reality proved otherwise.

The team that executed the acquisition of Preh consisted of three persons, i.e. Wang Jianfeng (Jeff), Guo Zhiming, and Cai Zhengxin. "We were crossing the river by feeling the stones," recalled Guo and Cai. A growth strategy surfaced during discussions with the Preh management team. The support of Preh's managers was key for the success of the acquisition and the subsequent development of the business.

Michael Roesnick was president and CEO of Preh GmbH from 1999 until he retired in 2016. He was at the company when it was absorbed by DBAG and then by Joyson Electronics. When interviewed by the Chinese media following the transaction, he reflected on selecting Joyson Electronics as Preh's partner/owner. "The management of Preh GmbH were very supportive of this transaction. We saw significant opportunities for our new team, particularly in regard to the rapid development of our business in China. With Joyson Electronics' help, we were able to get a foothold in the Chinese market more easily. Preh's financial strength was also fortified. These advantages will help accelerate Preh's development. Cultural differences withstanding, we were open and eager to learn from each other. But the truth is we were luckily not starting from scratch, as we had known each other for 3 years already."

According to Rolf Scheffels, then chairman of the supervisory board of Preh and a board member of DBAG, the invitation extended by Joyson Electronics during the negotiation that the both sides should develop the Chinese market together fitted Preh's business perfectly and was ideal for taking the German automotive supplier to the next stage of its development to have a significant presence in all major markets i.e. Asian, Europe, and US. According to the arrangement with Joyson Electronics, Preh could largely retain its organizational structure and was therefore able to benefit from the synergy effect almost immediately after the transaction.

6.3 Integration and Transformation

As one can imagine, employees at acquired companies would worry about the consequences of the takeover. Customers would be concerned likewise, when the acquired firms in question deliver critical technology to them, as in the case of Preh. For example, its high-profile customers including BMW and Audi were anxious about the possibility that the new shareholder would leak their technology to the competitors. Confronted with challenges from a variety of frontiers including legal regulations, management issues, and cultural differences etc., Joyson Electronics managed to find its own solutions, as there was no ready playbook to follow.

6.3.1 From "Preh Is Still Preh" to "Preh Is a Member of the Joyson Electronics Family"

In 2005, Beijing No. 1 Machine Tool Plant acquired the German firm Coburg, a global leader in heavy machine tools. To address the German employees' concerns about losing their jobs, Beijing No. 1 embraced an approach to be followed by many other Chinese acquirers in the years to come. Anything but dictating the way forward, Beijing No. 1 decided not to participate in the operations directly, but let the incumbent management team continue to run the business. "Beijing No. 1 was a role model for us at that time", said Guo Zhiming, "Back then, both sides agreed that our roles would remain the same. We decided that Preh would still be Preh and the existing management team, which boasted more than a decade of experience on average, should stay in office. The senior managers did a good job bridging the employees the and new shareholder and helping building trust throughout the entire organization. It was also important for staff that there was a smooth transition period following the acquisition, as they weren't sure what would happen once they were taken over by a Chinese investor."

Joyson Electronics decided to continue on the course set by the original owner, DBAG, and waited to restructure the management team till the next year. Following the adjustment, the new five-person management team consisted of the old Preh GmbH team members with the addition of Cai Zhengxin, the only representative of Joyson Electronics on the team. Based in the headquarters of Preh in Bad Neustadt an der Saale, Cai was to facilitate communication between Joyson Electronics and Preh, and more importantly help develop the business in China. He later took on the role of chief supply chain officer, responsible for procurement, supply chain, and commercial vehicles. In 2012, Jochen Ehrenberg was also promoted to the management team.

As typical of medium-sized German companies, Preh GmbH does not have a board of directors and only has a supervisory board composed of six people. As stipulated by law, there were two staff representatives on the board, while the other four people members were Chairman of the Board Wang Jianfeng and Guo Zhiming, both from Joyson Electronics; Willibert Schleuter, an expert in automotive parts; and Rolf Scheffels, member of the board of Preh's former major shareholder DBAG.

At the end of 2015, Preh's CEO, Michael Roesnick retired after 16 years of service for the company. Christoph Hummel, responsible for sales and marketing, stepped up as CEO, while Roesnick took a seat on the supervisory board as chairman of the board. Ernst-Rudolf, responsible for finance, retired in May 2016. Rui Marques Dias took his place. Cai Zhengxin continued to serve on the management team, while Stavros Mitrakis joined the board from Panasonic Automotive & Industrial Systems Europe and has been responsible for Preh's Car Connect business unit since 2017 (built around TechniSat Automotive, which was acquired in 2016). Preh GmbH has now completed its first managerial restructuring since the acquisition.

Being a leader in several niche markets, the German manufacturer demonstrates one of the most distinct characteristics of hidden champions, namely the continuity of their management teams. The chairman of the original management board was in office for 16 years, and the CFO was in his role for 20 years. The loyalty to the company was not only limited to the boardroom. "Many of our employees are the second or even the third generation in their families to work at our company. At our annual parties, I got to meet employees that have been working at Preh GmbH for 25, 40, or even 50 years," said Guo, amazed by the phenomenon that was rarely seen in China.

As cooperation deepens, the boundaries between Preh GmbH and Joyson Electronics become blurred. Although Preh continues to be a separate entity, the whole company, particularly the management team, have begun to see themselves as part of the Joyson Electronics family.

6.3.2 Employee Evaluation and Incentives

As in virtually all M&A's, trust is a key factor to tap the potential and maximize the synergy. Before the acquisition, Joyson Holding and Preh established a foundation of mutual trust during their meetings in China and Germany, and after the takeover, mutual trust became a central pillar of successful cooperation, as Joyson Electronics entrusted Preh's incumbent management team with running and developing the business.

While granting Preh quasi full autonomy in its operations, Joyson Electronics took great care in motivating and empowering the management team. Vice President Guo, who had been safeguarding the acquisition and was now in charge of Human Resources for the group, spent several months discussing development plans and KPI's with the German team. In addition, a dedicated team at Joyson Electronics went to great lengths to identify best practices through different avenues on how to set meaningful KPIs for the management of the acquired firm.

In line with the 2011 transaction plan, Joyson Electronics issued stock to buy the 74.9% of shares in Preh Holding (which held 94.9% of Preh GmbH shares) from Joyson Holding and the remaining 5.1% shares held by minority shareholders in Preh GmbH. Joyson Electronics paid the other seven Preh shareholders in cash for the remaining 25.1% of shares in Preh Holding (see Fig. 6.5). Consequently, Joyson Electronics had completely absorbed Preh GmbH and the incumbent management team no longer owned any equity in the company. Many analysts following Joyson Electronics red-flagged it as a major risk for the Chinese automotive supplier and questioned how Joyson Electronics would be able to retain the key persons now that they were no longer invested in the company. There was also concern that while Preh might contribute to group revenue for a year or two, it stood the risk of becoming a shell company, if the management team were gone. To address the concerns of the

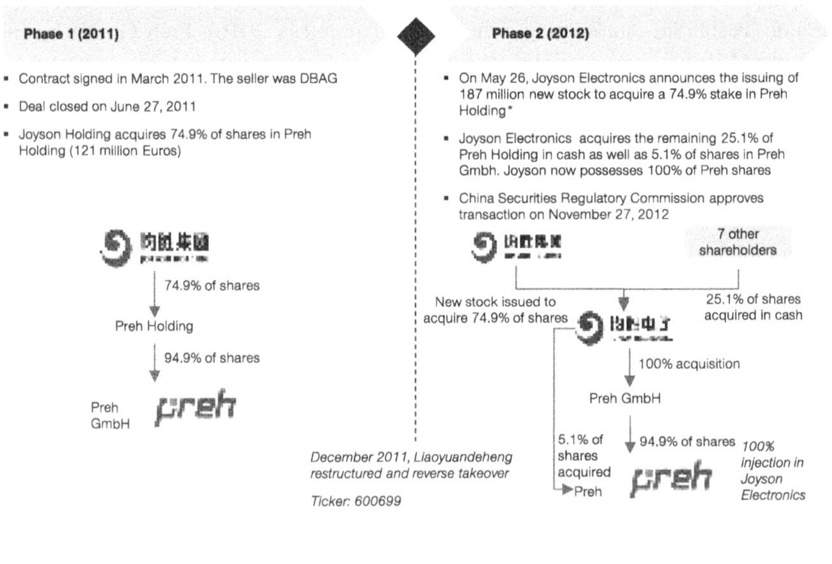

*Worth 180 million euros. The main reasons for the premium are: 1. its low valuation due to the financial crisis when Joyson Electronics first acquired the company; 2. the price estimation included the advisory and consulting fees; 3. from 2011 to 2012, almost a year and a half's revenue was attributed to the listed company; 4. the currency exchange losses were borne by Joyson Electronics; 5: the contract to acquire the 5.1% of shares included cost of 3% annual interest rate.

Fig. 6.5 Two phases of the Preh GmbH transaction. Source: Joyson Electronics

investors, Joyson Electronics announced a so-called Management Participation Program, according to which the management would be rewarded with shares in June 2013. More specifically:

- Joyson Electronics agreed to sell 1.938% of shares in Preh worth 4.68 million euros in total to the five board members (Michael Roesnick, Ernst-Rudolf Bauer, Christoph Hummel, Cai Zhengxin, and Jochen Ehrenberg) and to NES MPP GmbH & Co. KG, a company owned by 24 Preh middle-level managers, with terms of limitation fixing the seller and the buyer in the transaction
- The shares of the five board members account for 66% of the shares sold; NES MPP owns the remaining 34%
- Joyson Electronics would buy back the shares at a premium if the performance of the company and the management team meets pre-defined targets

"In order to incentivize the management team, we sold them some shares in Preh. If performance is good in 5 years' time, we will buy the shares back. We believe we are the first Chinese company to do so. The incentives were supposed to reward and enhance overall competence in sales, R&D etc., and not limit the focus to pure financial targets such as revenue and profit," commented Wang on the new reward mechanism.

Following the change in management, Preh Holding's revenue rose from 412 million euros in 2011 to 763 million euros in 2015 with a compound annual growth rate of 17%. In contrast, the compound annual growth rate of Preh from 2006 to 2010 was 6% before the acquisition by Joyson Electronics. In 2015, Preh reaped net profit of 47.48 million euros.

In 2016, Joyson Electronics and Preh jointly acquired TechniSat GmbH's automotive division, which specialized in infotainment systems, navigation, connectivity, and telematics. The strategy was to integrate it into Preh's automotive electronics business unit, leading to transformation of Preh's organizational structure. As a result, the existing reward mechanism for the Preh managers was no longer appropriate and the management decided to terminate it. By now, Preh's revenue had increased from under 400 million to 840 million euros, with new orders worth 200 million euros in the backlog. On April 13, 2016, Joyson Electronics bought back the 1.938% of shares for almost 20 million euros. In merely 3 years, the management team's shares were now worth four times as much as when they bought them. The buy-back measure did not end there, however. Joyson Electronics and Preh management have promised to speak to the key persons and employee representatives in order to design a new reward mechanism that ensures the automotive electronics business continues along its rapid growth trajectory.

6.3.3 Continuous Investment in R&D

Joyson Electronics acquired Preh to gain access to technology and upgrade its product offerings. Joyson Electronics and Preh went to great lengths to develop new products in automotive electronics, such as the smart central control system for the Lincoln MKZ series and the iDrive Touch for the BMW 7, which debuted at the Shanghai International Automobile Industry Exhibition in 2013.

In its financial books throughout the recent years, Joyson Electronics' management emphasized the importance of R&D. Looking back at its 20 years of history, it is apparent that its continuous investment in R&D has been a decisive factor in Joyson Electronics' success. According to the research by Simon (2012), regular companies generally invest around 3% of their revenue in R&D, while companies on the Global 1000 list invest 3.6% on average. Hidden champions, in contrast, would invest up to 6% of their turnover. In 2015, Joyson Electronics invested over 6% in R&D activities. From 2012 to 2016, the compound annual growth rate of its investment on R&D was 66%. According to Preh's chief supply chain officer, Cai Zhengxin, Preh has always attached great importance to R&D and has invested 9% annually in recent years, which is even higher than the average of the group as a whole.

In 2013, there were more than 1000 employees in Joyson Electronics' R&D team, out of whom 60% are in Germany and the remainder in China. Such a high level of investment in R&D human resources ensures that the company's core competencies are maintained and further developed. In the meantime, Joyson Electronics spared no efforts to attract skilled staff in China and abroad. It formed close partnerships with leading educational institutes including the University of Michigan, the University of Würzburg, Tongji University, and Zhejiang University's College of Mechanical Engineering to foster future talents for the company. As of 2016, Joyson Electronics has established three research centers worldwide, specializing in product design, software development, and data processing. Over 2000 people and counting are employed in R&D, as Joyson Electronics leadership set their minds on building a leading technology-driven company (Fig. 6.6).

In only half a decade, revenue at Joyson Electronics increased from 3.3 billion in 2011 to 18.6 billion yuan in 2016, with a compound annual growth rate of 40%. Both internal growth and external expansion have helped Joyson Electronics rise to a large-scale automotive supplier. According to the company's business plan, Joyson Electronics will build a global R&D center in China in 2017. The R&D center of Preh Car Connect and KSS Active Safety in China will also be expanded to accelerate the penetration of their technology into the Chinese market. In the future, all product lines will be more closely linked and integrated, establishing the company's position as an integrated solution provider for the automotive industry.

6.3.4 Exploring the New Markets

After the acquisition of Preh GmbH, Joyson Electronics helped its German daughter company strengthen its foothold in the Asia-Pacific and North America, sharing customers and channels to the benefit of both sides. At first, the company equipped essentially German vehicles but later expanded to US vehicles from manufacturers such as Ford and General Motors. Now the company has a powerful clientele featuring Audi, BMW, Daimler, Ford, General Motors, Porsche, Volkswagen, among others.

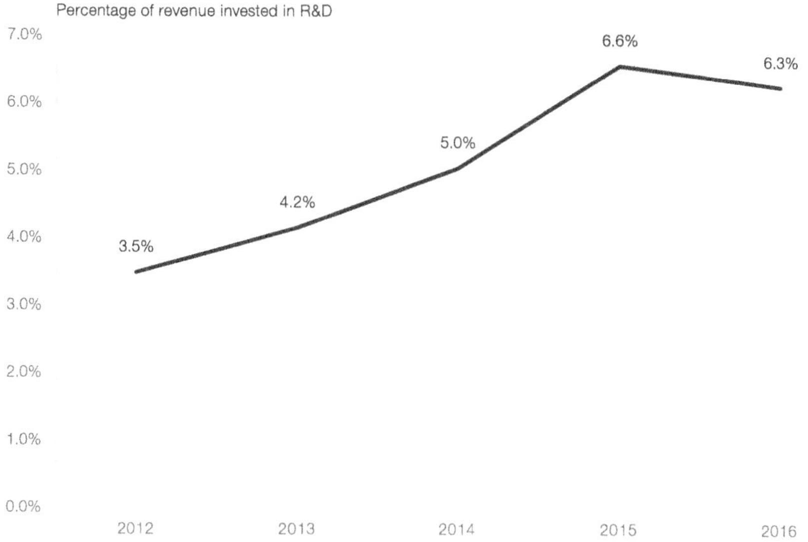

Fig. 6.6 The percentage of revenue invested in R&D by Joyson Electronics (2012–2016). Source: Joyson Electronics

Departing from Preh's reliance on the European market, Joyson Electronics ramped up its activities in China, the biggest automobile market, by localizing and re-innovating German technology. A case in point was the cooperation with Tongji University to localize the technology in battery management systems. With the local advantages and the support of Joyson Electronics, the Ningbo Preh-Joyson joint venture has managed to double its revenue year after year.

Since 2012, 70% of Joyson Electronics' revenue has been generated internationally, solidifying its position as a global player. By sharing technology, customers, and channels, exploiting markets jointly, and developing new products independently but in a coordinated way, Joyson Electronics and Preh have been able to grow their gross margins (Fig. 6.7).

At closing of the acquisition, market analysts were not in full agreement about whether the transaction would pay off. After 5 years, Joyson Electronics proved itself by registering a stellar performance and showcasing the efficacy of a well-devised strategy. Its stock price has consistently beaten the Shanghai composite index over years. Before the acquisition, Joyson Electronics had a market cap of about 1 billion yuan. Its market value had risen to 30 billion yuan by the end of the first quarter of 2017 (Fig. 6.8).

6.3.5 Integration of Culture and Management

Integration hinges on cooperation in many ways. "In the integration phase, we recognized the potential risk of disagreements because of cultural and managerial

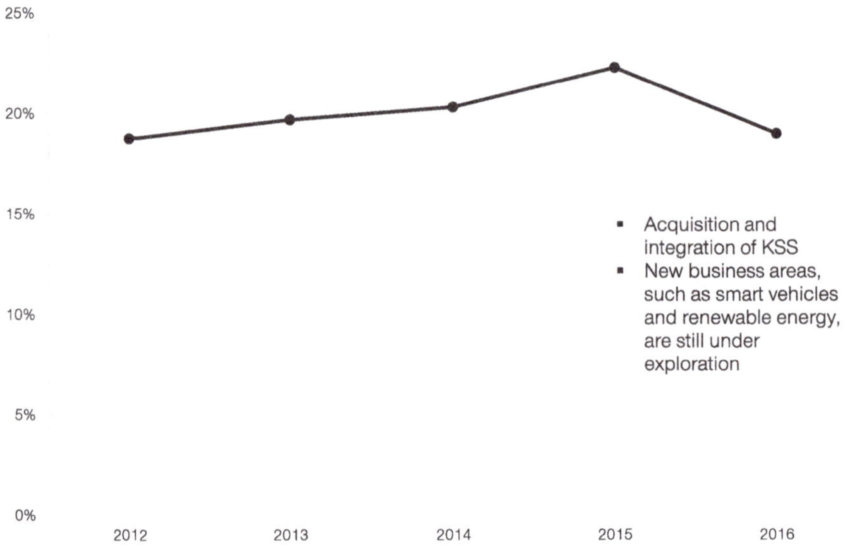

Fig. 6.7 Gross margin growth of Joyson Electronics (2012–2016). Source: Joyson Electronics

Fig. 6.8 Joyson Electronics share price development (2011–2017). Source: Sina Finance

differences. Therefore, it was important to build trust between us. The best way to solve problems is by understanding one another and communicating. Sometimes, you have to be able to compromise." As the representative of Joyson Electronics on the Preh management team, Cai Zhengxin has lots to say about the challenges the company tackled during the integration.

Shortly after the acquisition, Joyson Electronics suggested that Preh should shut down the production site in Romania, reasoning that production costs in China would be much lower. However, the Preh management team insisted that one should not only look at the numbers. There were other factors that should be considered. For example, the Romanian plant was logistically easy to reach and close to the R&D sites in Germany. The communication cost was also much lower, as many Romanian engineers were fluent in German. Moreover, Romania-made products could be labeled with the quality seal "Made in Europe". These arguments convinced Joyson's board. Not only did Preh keep the site, the production has since scaled up remarkably, with headcount shooting up from 100 to about 800.

The two sides did have conflicting opinions of the right strategy for China. Preh thought annual double-digit growth in the Chinese market was not realistic and that they should be more cautious with market expansion, which, in turn, had impact on allocation of resources and talent recruitment etc. "We said that we would prove it to them that our China strategy was realistic." said Guo. "In fact, even our plans were too conservative in hindsight. Preh wanted to hire a set number of employees for China according to the conventional business plan, the way that they were used to in Germany. However, China has its own peculiarities. It is a rapid developing market compared to Germany and in large cities, such as Shanghai and Beijing, staff are much more prone to change jobs. We insisted that we needed to hire extra people to factor in the potential churns and even agreed to bear the additional costs to appease Preh in the end. Time tells that we were right."

The German media and other companies were accusing Chinese investors of only being interested in getting their hands on German technology. Ran Peng, technical director from Joyson Preh Electronics refuted, "In many technological fields, Chinese firms are less advanced than German firms, but the Chinese market has immense and growing potential. Although Germany has advanced technology, its market is at a saturation point. The application of German technology should not be classed as a "transfer of technology"; we consider it unleashing the due potential of the German technology in the Chinese market." Following the acquisition, the German and Chinese R&D departments of Preh and Joyson Electronics have been working closely with and learning from each other and strengthening cooperation.

To support product development, particularly for electric vehicles, Joyson Electronics has provided Preh with strategic directives and financial aid but respects it as an independent business in the meantime. Joyson stressed to its new daughter company that as China was developing rapidly, it was important to invest in marketing, R&D, and customer relations. "Joyson Electronics' key strengths are the ability to make right judgment calls on market developments and having deep understanding of the biggest vehicle market in the world, while Preh excels at planning and executing strategy. We have made the best use of our strengths and made up for our weaknesses. This is the principle of our and any successful cooperation," emphasized Cai.

"The Germans and the Chinese have become one team. German used to be the business language at Preh, but now both companies have adopted English as the official company speak," said Guo. Today, around 20 Chinese employees work on projects on average at one time in Germany and more than 10 experienced engineers with over 10 years work experience are based out of Ningbo, 200 km away from metropolitan

Shanghai. The best of the two world are joined together: The skills in innovation and quality control from Germany and the financial means and market savvy from China.

Apparently, there were also differences in modus operandi. "Germans are bound to make and stick to a detailed plan about just everything, whereas Chinese are used to moving plans around situations," noted Huang Yonghao, deputy general manager of Joyson Preh IMA, "For example, the Germans will discuss the time and the agenda of the next meeting during the current meeting, which was unheard of for us. Over time, we learn to appreciate the approach and found it actually a good way to improve efficiency and adopted the same at Joyson Electronics. Another habit our Ningbo staff picked up from Preh is to plan meetings for the coming year with the topics and participant list far in advance."

The best practices passed on from the Germans have honed Joyson Electronics' competencies in managing international businesses, which was a major step forward for the company. Proposal processes and calculation tools have been optimized and SAP has been introduced as the company's management system. Furthermore, Joyson Electronics has learned how to calculate budgets and process data more accurately.

6.3.6 From "Crossing the River by Feeling the Stone" to "Leveraging the Know-How"

There is consensus both internally and externally that the acquisition of Preh GmbH was a game changer for Joyson Electronics, which has led to remarkable accumulation and assimilation of knowledge and accelerated growth in international markets. R&D, production, and sales have spread over Europe, the United States, and Asia and its growth has accelerated ever since. Since 2013, Joyson Electronics has conducted a series of successful overseas acquisitions building on the success of Preh, including Innoventis, a software company; IMA, a manufacturer of automated machinery; QUIN, a supplier of high-end steering wheels and interior and exterior decoration; KSS, an American vehicle safety company, TechniSat Automotive, an information system supplier; and EVANA, an industrial robots and automation manufacturer.

In the cases of Innoventis (2013), IMA (2014) and EVANA (2016), the core members of the acquisition team came from Preh GmbH, which also acted as a conduit for the transaction. In the case of TechniSat Automotive, Preh cooperated with Joyson Electronics early on in the acquisition, and in the due diligence and integration phase, Preh played an even more prominent role, contributing valuable advice and insights to complete the transaction.

"Joyson Electronics' team in Germany is undoubtedly the team with the most experience in the field of Sino-German M&A's," said Liu Yuan, vice president of Joyson Electronics. "Our team are often solicited by venture capitalists and Chinese firms wanting to invest in Germany, which showcases that our achievements in the past years are well recognized by the market."

When it first engaged with Preh GmbH in 2011, Joyson Electronics was crossing the river by feeling the stones, relying on its hunch of the big picture of future trends.

Today, after living through so many overseas acquisitions with trial and error, Joyson Electronics has sharpened its global growth strategy and begun to leverage its acquired know-how.

6.4 Growth Initiatives

In 2012, just after the acquisition of Preh, Joyson Electronics' business had four pillars, i.e. auto electronics, interior and exterior accessories, functional parts, and industrial automation equipment. In 2014, the interior and exterior accessories and functional parts were merged and battery management systems (BMS) was officially added to the business portfolio. In addition to serving BMW, the BMS department also worked with prestigious industry players, such as Tesla and China South Locomotive & Rolling Stock Corporation Limited (Fig. 6.9).

In addition to robust organic growth, Joyson Electronics continued its shopping spree in 2016. It acquired KSS and TS Automotive, adding two more automotive electronics business units to its portfolio: auto safety through KSS; and auto connectivity through its division Preh Car Connect, which TS Automotive was incorporated into.

The year 2016 was a period of transition for Joyson Electronics. Old product lines were upgraded through two acquisitions and the company geared up for transforming itself into a comprehensive technology provider. From the product perspective, Joyson Electronics has covered the four important aspects of driving, namely, human–machine interface, vehicle safety (both active and passive), infotainment, and connectivity, and even assumes leading positions in these areas worldwide, making the company a rising global champion (Fig. 6.10).

6.4.1 Vehicle Safety

On June 8, 2016 Joyson Electronics completed the acquisition of KSS for 920 million dollars, corresponding to a P/E ratio of 56. According to people familiar with the matter, Joyson Electronics also planned to inject another 100 million dollars into KSS to improve its finances and fund new businesses. KSS specializes in active and passive vehicle safety and has established itself as a premium supplier since the 1950s. Its offerings include airbags, seat belts, seat belt pre-tensioners, steering wheels, and inflators, etc.

Following the acquisition, the company went on to optimize the active vehicles safety and smart driving systems business. Three R&D centers were built—in the United States, China, and Korea respectively—which work closely together on specific product lines. For its relatively new active safety products, KSS has received new orders worth more than 120 million dollars and in addition to its existing global customers, the company has also won new customers in China, such as Geely, Aichiyiwei, NextEV, and Changfeng Motor. Cooperation projects are currently under way with Shanghai Volkswagen, Changan, and Beijing Automotive.

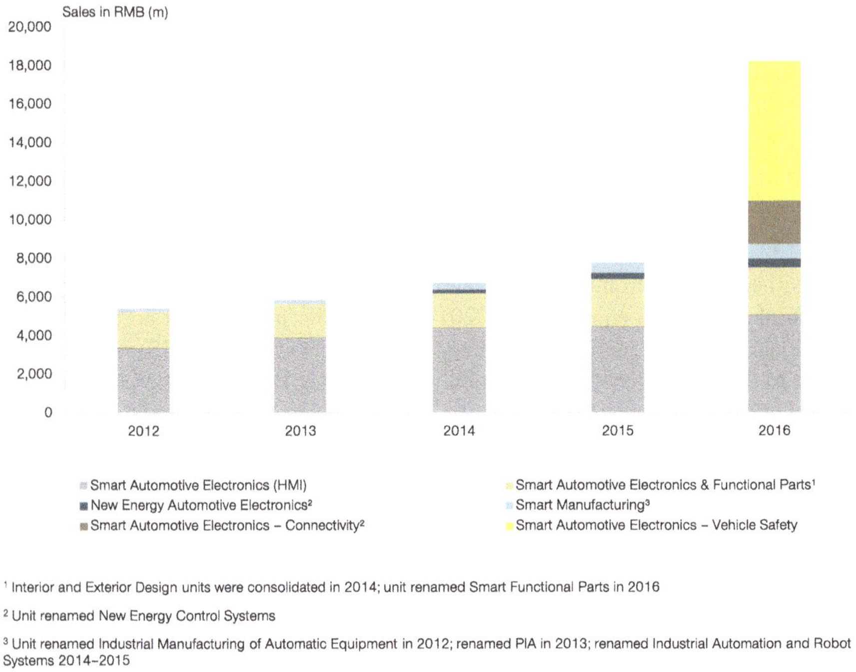

Fig. 6.9 Joyson Electronics product lines and their revenue (2012–2016). Source: Joyson Electronics

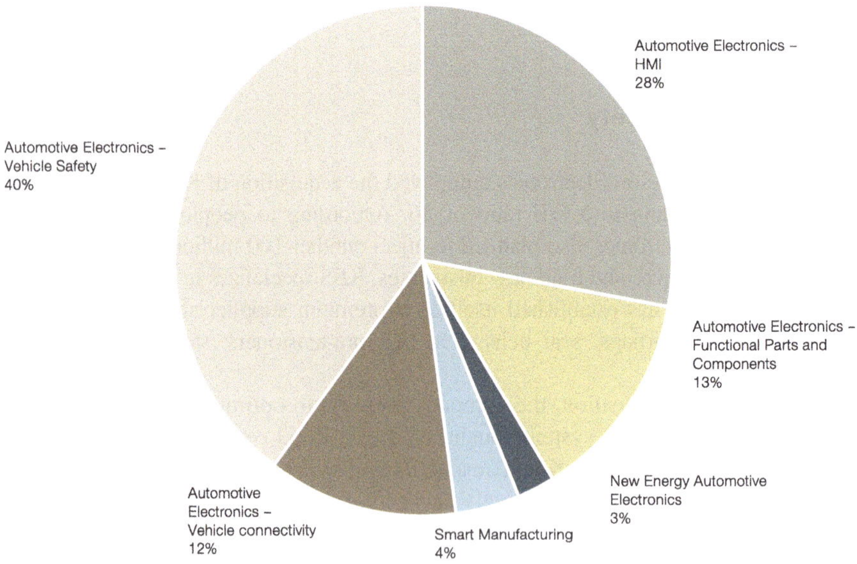

Fig. 6.10 Joyson Electronics' business units (2016). Source: Joyson Electronics

6.4.2 Vehicle Connectivity

On March 4, 2016 Joyson Electronics took over TS Automotive for 180 million euros, representing a P/E ratio of 18. TS Automotive was part of TS Daun and focused on vehicle information systems, more specifically data interaction and liquid-crystal display (LCD) technology. Its main products include infotainment systems, navigation, assisted driving, and vehicle connectivity systems. It provides a variety of comprehensive solutions to car manufacturers and is a core supplier to the Volkswagen Group.

TS Automotive was integrated into Preh, following which a new business unit Preh Car Connect (PCC) emerged. PCC complements Preh's existing human–machine interface (HMI) business with state-of-the-art automotive electronics such as vehicle-to-everything (V2X) technology. Joyson Electronics' innovative products based on augmented reality (AR) technology, e.g. head-up displays (HUD), are also on the verge of commercialization. They will be integrated in the central console and as such an important addition to HMI. In the future, Joyson Electronics will be able to provide more centralized control platforms along with PCC's solutions.

In total, the connectivity business generated revenue of 2.25 billion yuan. Its gross margin was 11.9%, increasing considerably from 8.3% in the first half of 2016. As the integration process proceeds, profitability is expected to improve further.

6.4.3 Human–Machine Interface

The HMI informs drivers of speed, mileage, maintenance, road conditions, etc. in real time and enables them to control the navigation system, air conditioning, Bluetooth, and stereo configurations all from one place. The most commonly seen HMI systems include BMW's iDrive, Mercedes-Benz's COMAND, Audi's MMI, Volvo's Sensus, and Toyota's Remote Touch, etc. HMI is Preh GmbH's flagship division and it drives Joyson Electronics' business in this area.

Preh now focuses on a number of market segments, including central controls, steering wheel switches, and center stacks, and multi-touch has become one of the company's core technologies. In addition, Joyson Electronics acquired and integrated QUIN, a specialist in interiors and high-end products, such as steering wheel solutions in 2014, in the hope to tap synergy with Preh's existing HMI technology. The subsequent acquisition of TS Automotive in 2016 expanded Preh's HMI business into connectivity and complementing Preh's HMI offerings.

Nowadays, Joyson Electronics' HMI business offers three main product lines: driving control systems, air-conditioning control systems, and steering wheel controllers. Joyson Electronics achieved revenue of 5.1 billion yuan from HMI in 2016, or an increase of 14.1% year on year, while its gross margin increased to 24.6%.

6.4.4 Interior and Exterior Accessories

Originally, Joyson Electronics made and marketed automotive interiors and exteriors. The core products included windshield wipers, air conditioning vents, and engine intake manifolds for German car makers such as FAW-VW and Shanghai VW as well as automotive suppliers like Yanfeng Visteon Automotive and Faurecia. As the growth of the automotive industry slows down, competition is becoming fiercer and price pressure is rising, which caused gross margin to shrink between 2012 and 2014.

In an effort to improve the profitability of its interior and exterior accessories business, Joyson Electronics has revamped its product lineup and leaned towards developing new higher-end functional parts. In 2014, Joyson Electronics acquired QUIN, a company specializing in luxury interiors, and started its global strategy to upgrade its interior and exterior product portfolio. The following year, in order to re-allocate resources to advanced technology, the company carved out its shares in Dehua and carved out commodity-like products from its portfolio.

Soon after, Joyson decided to expand its functional parts division aimed at the Asian and North American markets. In the US, General Motors awarded it a project to produce air conditioning vents, while the other two big players Ford and Chrysler initiated cooperation with Joyson Electronics. In Europe, production was inaugurated in Romania to supply parts to customers located in Europe, while in China, the company won the "Excellent Supplier" award from heavy weights like FAW-Volkswagen and Beijing Mercedes-Benz.

In 2016, Joyson's functional parts division achieved revenue of 2.45 billion yuan, down by 1.7% compared to last year due to carve-out of Shanghai Huade, while gross margin improved by 5% points (see Fig. 6.11).

6.4.5 Battery Management Systems for New-Energy Vehicles

Battery management systems act as important interfaces between electric cars and their batteries. Some of the main functions are monitoring the battery's status in real-time, conducting online diagnoses and generating maintenance forecasts, assessing the state of charge, and controlling balance and heat management. Being a core technology of new-energy vehicles (NEV's), the BMS ensures batteries remain within their safe operating parameters and keep the NEV's running properly.

BMS used to be a subsidiary of Preh's sensor business, however, with the rapid development of NEV's, Joyson Electronics came to realize the vast potential of this sector. After a lengthy period of convincing and negotiating, the management decided to spin off BMS from Preh as an independent strategic unit and a special R&D center was also established.

Preh is BMW's sole supplier of battery management systems worldwide. Mercedes-Benz (48 V system project), Porsche (electric vehicle project), and Tesla are also its customers. In the China market, Joyson Electronics BMS's customers include Chery, Geely, and Shanghai VW. In 2016, Joyson also won the order from

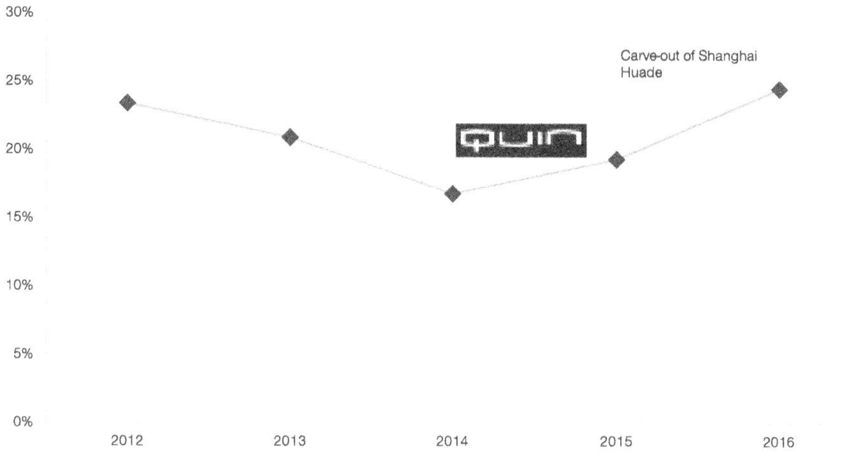

Fig. 6.11 Gross margin of Joyson Electronics' functional parts business (2012–2016). Source: Joyson Electronics

Geely to develop a new generation of hybrid car platform. Great Wall Motors, Changan Automobile, and Beijing Automobile Works complement the list of promising prospects in China.

In 2016, Preh and Qualcomm entered into a contract to jointly develop and market Halo wireless electric vehicle charging technology (WEVC) for use in hybrid and electric cars. In the same year, BMS achieved revenue of 443 million yuan, an increase of 48.6% over the previous year. Gross margin was 17.42%, slightly higher than in 2015.

6.4.6 Smart Manufacturing

In 2015, 248,000 industrial robots were sold globally, out of which 66,000 were in China, making China the biggest market for robots worldwide. However, there were less than 30 robots per 10,000 people in China, i.e. less than half the global average, implying great growth potential. Digitalizing, networking, and smart manufacturing based on new technologies and optimized production processes will become a megatrend in the next 5–10 years in China.

Launched in 1982, Preh's innovative automated production lines can manufacture, assemble, and test products according to customers' individual demands. In addition to internal use, Preh also supplied to leading automotive suppliers like Bosch, Siemens, TRW Automotive, Lear Corporation, and ZF Friedrichshafen, etc. In 2014, Joyson Electronics acquired another German machinery company, IMA, to strengthen its robotics business. Immediately after, Preh's automation business was spun off and integrated with IMA to form Preh IMA Automation GmbH (PIA). In 2015, Joyson Electronics and Preh formed Ningbo Joyson Preh Industrial Automation & Robot Co., Ltd. (JPIA) with equal ownership. The aim of JPIA was to explore the Chinese market and serve the clients from the vicinity. In May 2016, PIA acquired the US firm EVANA, which specialized in industrial robots and automation, automotive solutions, and technical consulting. Its customers are from the automotive, manufacturing, health care, and medical industries.

In 2016, Joyson Electronics completed the acquisition of KSS and TS Automotive, strengthening its automotive electronics business. However, this had a side effect on its smart manufacturing activities. The major customers in this business line, such as Bosch, Continental, and ZF-Friedrichshafen expressed concerns about the potential conflict of interest with Preh. According to the company's financial figures, smart manufacturing only generated revenue of 757 million yuan in 2016. Not including EVANA's revenue of 157 million, this only equates to an increase of 47 million yuan over last year, while net profit dropped in the same time period.

To preempt a negative long-term impact on the group as a whole, Joyson Electronics made a sudden but understandable announcement in April 2017 to carve out the smart manufacturing business and transfer 50% of its shares in JPIA to Preh IMA Automation GmbH. At the same time, all shares in Preh IMA Automation were being transferred to PIA Automation Holding GmbH registered in Frankfurt, whose main shareholder is Joyson Holding's subsidiary, Ningbo Preh Automation Ltd.

6.4.7 Autonomous Vehicles

Joyson Electronics' 2016 financial statement foresaw autonomous vehicles to be the future of the automotive industry worldwide. For this reason, driverless technology, new energy systems, and connectivity will be the primary focus of R&D for the company in the next 5–10 years.

According to a 2015 book by Goldman Sachs on the commercialization of self-driving cars, autonomous vehicles would change the automotive landscape, bringing a myriad of challenges and opportunities in the coming years. In 2015, the market volume of Advanced Driver Assistance Systems (ADAS) was approximately 3 billion dollars. By 2025, the market volume of ADAS/AV is expected to increase to 96 billion dollars and by 2030, this figure will be almost 200 billion dollars.

Based on over a decade of market experience in China and navigating international markets, Joyson Electronics has developed three business areas that will be key in the future: autonomous vehicles, safety and the connectivity (Table 6.1).

Table 6.1 Key future business areas for Joyson Electronics

Phase of automation	Automatic driving	Vehicle safety	Entertainment
Market potential (2021)	39.6 billion euros	49.3 billion euros	13.4 billion euros
Compound annual growth rate	33%	27%	18%
Development trends	• The fastest-growing area tor the connectivity business unit • Many technologies are developing faster than expected • High demand in the Chinese market	• Global demand will increase due to the growth of the Chinese market • Regulations making eCall rapid assistance systems a legal requirement will encourage investment	• Customer preferences are changing, particularly in Asia; entertainment is increasingly important • Integrated with smart phones and individual wearable devices • Digitalization will promote inter-industrial coordination and integration
Main products	• Automatic parking; low-speed navigation in traffic jams (in operation) • Automatic, long-distance, and high-speed navigation (expected 2020–2025)	• Automatic alarm system for accidents • Danger warning system for hazardous situations; barrier/blind-spot evasion devices • Safety systems for collisions: automatic acceleration or steering wheel to prevent accidents	• Personalized entertainment, such as social media, music and film libraries, restaurant guides, etc. • Wi-Fi hotspot technology allowing the vehicle to function as an office and provide connectivity during meetings, etc.
Challenges	• Regulations unclear • Legal compliance issues	• The commercialization of these products is limited after standardization	• No standard process • Competition for controlling point • Automobile manufactures have to adapt quickly to the electronics industry

Source: US's National Highway Traffic Safety Administration

6.5 Closing Remarks

Joyson Electronics has come a long way since its foundation in 2004, achieving revenue of almost 20 billion yuan in just 12 years. During this time, Joyson overcame many challenges to become an international group with a clear vision for the future. Its model of "internal growth and external expansion" has made good use of the capital market and helped Joyson Electronics develop its core competencies.

Unlike many Chinese companies, Joyson Electronics has fostered a global perspective early on. The acquisition and integration of Preh was Joyson Electronics' first major attempt in expanding its footprint worldwide. This marked the beginning of a journey of internationalizing its resources and positioning itself as a major global supplier of automotive electronics, which in turn helped Joyson Electronics improve its management competencies and generate remarkable return for its shareholders.

Looking back over the 12 years of development, Joyson Electronics' management team identifies three important factors that ensured the success of its business:

- Investing in technology and R&D over the long-term, including internal investment and the optimization and expansion of global resources
- Clearly delineating "cash cow" and "star" businesses and adequately allocating resources between the two to optimize future benefit
- Developing the Chinese market: Joyson Electronics' acceptance of new technology and the speed at which it integrates it has given the group a significant advantage

M&A's are an effective way of expanding globally, but proper integration of new business entities is critical to long-term success. For Joyson Electronics, 2017 is a time for integration. An R&D center for KSS safety and Preh cars is being developed in China to accelerate the integration of the technology and further strengthen its position in the Chinese market. Joyson Electronics' own global R&D center will also be developed in China to integrate its various product lines and make the company a solution provider.

In 2017, mature business units, such as the HMI and car safety division, will be integrated and further developed, in order to capture a larger share of the global market. In its new business areas, the current scale of investment will be maintained and cooperation will be deepened with up- and down-stream partners. For the self-driving and Internet of Vehicles sector, new technologies are set to be commercialized and new customers will be found, opening the way for new innovative projects. Resource allocation is also set to be optimized, laying a solid foundation for long-term development.

Another focus for 2017 is the safety sector. The Japanese airbag supplier Takata is currently being dismantled after filing for bankruptcy, changing the global car safety landscape enormously. In order to make the most of this opportunity, Joyson Electronics will invest in its own production capabilities and grow its customer base. At the time of writing, Joyson has announced that it will take over Takata for 1.588 billion dollars without its toxic assets relating to its massive recall of airbags. Meanwhile, Joyson Holding is also starting to expand its automation portfolio. One of its subsidiaries, PIA, has recently acquired the Austrian automation company M&R.

Joyson Electronics is still a relatively young company. It has built a global group within a short time period. Chinese firms which intend to invest abroad often benchmark Joyson Electronics. When asked what will be the next big thing for

Joyson Electronics, a manager said, "We have a great blueprint in place. Now it is time to execute and optimize. It will be a big thing, if we can pull it off."

Reference[1]

Simon, H. (2012). Hidden Champions - Aufbruch nach Globalia: Die Erfolgsstrategien unbekannter Weltmarktführer.

[1]Apart from those indicated in the figures, the authors consulted some other sources as follows. It cannot be excluded that some references found on internet may not be included here for lack of explicit source.

CIMC-Ziegler: Sailing to New Shores 7

This case study was published with kind permission of the CIMC Group.

As the ancient Chinese saying goes, watched flowers never bloom, while unattended willows grow. A case in point for these wise words is CIMC's acquisition of the Albert Ziegler Group in Germany. When the deal became public in 2013, it was considered a good bargain, although at that stage there was no unanimous opinion within the CIMC group about the future role of Ziegler. However, it soon became clear that Ziegler would be a salient piece of CIMC's global growth blueprint.

Concerned by its dependence on a single business area, i.e. container manufacturing, CIMC's leadership decided to follow a diversification strategy in the early 2000s. Over the subsequent years, CIMC completed numerous M&A's, and continued scouting for new business opportunities around the world. The strategy proved to work. CIMC has emerged as an industrial behemoth with annual revenue of over 60 billion Chinese yuan, 60% of which is generated overseas. In stark contrast to its focus on container products several decades ago, today's business portfolio is much more diversified, including engineering services, logistics services, airport facilities, finance, fire trucks and rescue equipment, among others. CIMC's journey toward a global conglomerate continues, encountering new shores along the way. This case study focuses on one of its newest business areas, the fire truck and rescue equipment business, the backbone of which is formed by the Albert Ziegler Group.

Prior to becoming part of CIMC, Ziegler had a negligible presence in China. The Middle Kingdom never came across as a key market for Ziegler, selling merely a few dozen fire trucks to China over many decades through various agents based out of Hong Kong or elsewhere. After all, China was too remote a market and Ziegler barely had the resources or infrastructure to provide proper service to local Chinese customers. Nevertheless, in early 2015, little more than a year after the acquisition, Ziegler delivered 17 large multi-functional urban fire trucks to the Guangxi Nanning fire department. This was the first time that Ziegler had exported to the Chinese market in batches. As a matter of fact, 2015 turned out to be a groundbreaking year for Ziegler, as order entry from China surpassed 100 fire trucks. In the same year, CIMC acquired 30% ownership of

J. Y. Yang et al., *Chinese M&As in Germany*, Management for Professionals,
https://doi.org/10.1007/978-3-319-99405-5_7

China Fire Safety Enterprise (CFE) through an equity swap between Ziegler and CFE, the first Chinese firefighting company listed on the Hong Kong stock exchange. Its reduced stake in Ziegler aside, prospects for CIMC's fire truck and rescue equipment business improved greatly in light of the potential synergy between Ziegler and CFE.

Under the umbrella of CIMC, Ziegler also managed to resume its growth course on its home turf in Germany. A collusion scandal had left the former German market leader with only a 20% share of the market in 2013. A turnaround strategy was put to action immediately after CIMC took over. Two years later, Ziegler had regained market leadership, boosting its domestic market share to 35%.

Apparently, CIMC has even bigger ambitions for Ziegler and the firefighting business in general. At the time of writing, plans were being made for further expansion in China and Europe, as well as other key markets around the world.

7.1 Background

CIMC and Ziegler have taken very distinct paths since they were founded. The former came into being in the wake of China's Reform and Opening-Up Policy in the 1980s; the latter had a rich history as a family-run business spanning over 125 years in the southwest of Germany. In what follows, we give a brief account of the histories of both companies before their paths crossed.

Unlike many other large-scale state-owned corporations that carry "China" in their names, China International Marine Containers (Group) Ltd., or CIMC, was born out of a pioneering initiative to attract foreign investment as the Chinese government introduced the Reform and Opening-Up Policy in 1979. CIMC was established in 1980 as a Sino-foreign joint venture between the China Merchants' Steam Navigation Company and the East Asiatic Company from Denmark. Its main products at the time were standard 20-foot containers based on the technology provided by the Danish partner. The first general manager of the company was Mr. Moesgaard, a Danish national, who was joined by a few more of his compatriots on the board of directors. He held the office until 1986, 1 year before the China Ocean Shipping (Group) Company, commonly known as COSCO, acquired a minority equity stake in CIMC. At the first board meeting after COSCO's investment, an all-Chinese board of directors was elected and the direction of future growth was set: "Specialize in container manufacturing, and diversify into other businesses."

Starting out as a humble low-cost container manufacturer, CIMC grew rapidly and eventually overtook once uncontested market leaders Hyundai and Jindo, both from Korea, in 1996. Ever since, CIMC has been the well-recognized leader in the container-manufacturing industry worldwide. Presently, half of all containers manufactured globally are made by CIMC. Moreover, CIMC is the only container manufacturer in the world that can deliver the complete range of container products. Building on its success in this sector, CIMC gradually expanded its business scope to road transportation vehicles, heavy trucks, and then to adjacent industries, such as energy, chemical and liquid food equipment, airport facilities, marine engineering, and logistics services. Latterly, the company has also set foot in real estate development and financial services.

Table 7.1 CIMC's cross-border M&A projects (not exhaustive)

Time	Target company	Relevance
1998	Acquisition of Lumprex Suriname N.V.	Completed the first overseas acquisition
2003	Acquisition of Vanguard (USA)	Entered the semi-trailer markets of North America
2007	Acquisition of Marshall Lethlean (Australia)	Established a production base for semi-trailers in Australia
2007	Acquisition of Burg Industries (LAG; Hovrieka) (Netherlands)	Entered the semi-trailer and beer and beverage equipment industries
2008	Acquisition of TGE (Germany)	Gained EPC capabilities for LNG receiving stations and petrochemical industries
2011	Acquisition of Bassoe Technology (Sweden)	Completed the conceptual design and basic design for offshore products
2012	Acquisition of Verbus (UK)	Entered the overseas modular building market
2012	Acquisition of Ziemann (Germany)	Gained capabilities for turnkey brewery solutions and saccharification equipment
2013	Acquisition of Air Marrel (France)	Gained technology for airport lift platform trucks and vehicles
2013	Acquisition of Ziegler (Germany)	Entered the high-end firefighting and rescue vehicle industry
2014	Acquisition of listed company Pteris (Singapore)	Expanded into airport baggage handling systems, air cargo handling system, and other business areas

Source: CIMC

Throughout its history, CIMC has often entered new markets by acquiring companies with strategic assets to leapfrog over incumbents. The group was a serial investor in overseas assets with long-track records (see Table 7.1 for a selection of CIMC's Cross-border M&A's).

Container manufacturing was CIMC's sole business area at its inception in 1980. As the diversification strategy unfolded, container manufacturing accounted for little over half of its total revenue by 2012, declining to about one third by 2016. Through continuous acquisitions and organic growth, CIMC has grown into a global conglomerate with over 300 subsidiaries and more than 60,000 employees worldwide. Its R&D centers, manufacturing bases, sales, and service centers are scattered across 20 countries and regions. An impressive 60% of CIMC's revenue is generated outside of China (see Fig. 7.1 for the milestones of CIMC).

CIMC's airport facilities business unit is a leading global supplier of airport equipment and its sales volume of boarding bridges ranks number one in the world. The company made the world's first boarding bridge for the Airbus A380 and had the highest sales of airport shuttle buses in China. Despite being one of the smallest business units by revenue, airport facilities business shows greatest growth potential. Compared to CIMC, Ziegler looks back on a much longer history. The company was founded by its namesake Albert Ziegler in 1891 in Giengen an der Brenz in the Swabian Alb area of Germany. In the very early days, the company was primarily engaged in producing and selling hoses manufactured at its five hose-weaving mills with eight employees in production and two others taking care of commercial affairs. In the 1910s, a second

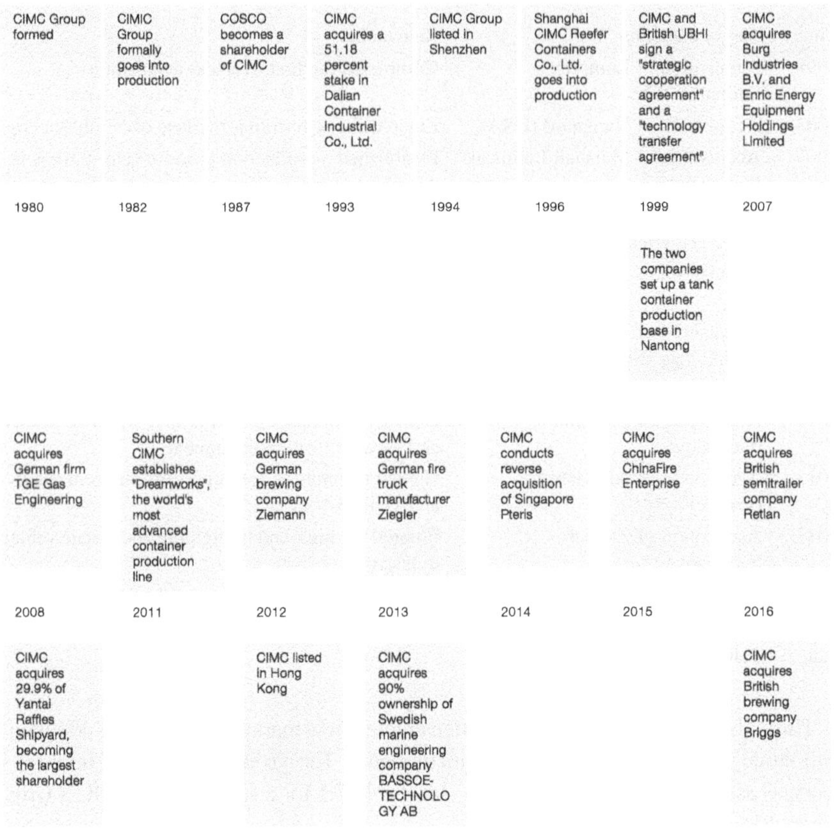

Fig. 7.1 Milestones of CIMC (1980–2016). Source: CIMC

product line, portable fire pumps, was added to the portfolio with the second generation of the founder's family at the helm. The first Ziegler fire truck was not produced until June 1953—a KLF 6 model built on an Opel-Blitz chassis (see Fig. 7.2), the prototype of which is still on exhibit in the corporate museum at Ziegler's facilities in Giengen an der Brenz.

Thanks to continuous innovation and marketing efforts, Ziegler rose to become a recognized and trusted brand in the firefighting business, building a sales network across several European markets. In addition to the production site in Giengen, Ziegler had production sites in Rendsburg and Mühlau in Germany, Winschoten in the Netherlands, Zagreb in Croatia, Bolzano in Italy, Seville in Spain, and Jakarta in Indonesia. Its current product portfolio consists of remodeled vehicles, such as standard and special fire vehicles; airport firefighting and rescue vehicles; traditional products, such as pumps and hoses; and accessories, including equipment, clothing, and spare parts.

Prior to its insolvency, Ziegler was one of the top five manufacturers of firefighting vehicles worldwide, and the biggest supplier in Germany by sales volume. The other

Fig. 7.2 KLF6, the first Ziegler fire truck. Source: Ziegler Group

main players in Germany were Iveco Magirus Brandschutztechnik, Rosenbauer, and Schlingmann. Together, the Big Four held about 90% of the German market.

At the beginning of 2011, German antitrust authorities imposed fines totaling 28 million euros on the four companies mentioned above for cartel practices following a 2-year investigation. It was determined that for several years, the four cartel members had been granting one another specific shares of sales, known as "target quotas", and had used a Switzerland-based accountant to transfer the profits. The accountant was believed to have been keeping logs to monitor adherence to the quotas agreed at the cartel's regular meetings at Zurich Airport. In addition to the Zurich meetings, sales managers at the four companies held regular meetings to allocate orders for firefighting vehicles from German municipalities among the cartel members. The four companies were also found to have concerted on price increases.

Ziegler was fined 8 million euros for its part in the cartel scandal. To make matters worse, many loyal customers suspended or canceled orders, when the scandal was exposed. After struggling with draining liquidity and a damaged reputation for more than 2 years, Ziegler's then CEO, who belonged to the fourth generation of the founding family, made the decision to file for insolvency in August 2011. The move caught many off guard and caused upheavals in the small town of Giengen, as Ziegler was the town's second largest employer with about 700 local employees. The Ziegler employees, in fear of losing their jobs, took to the streets to demonstrate against the insolvency application. Numerous townspeople and firefighters from surrounding neighborhoods also joined the demonstration to show support for the angry protesters, who believed that their company could still be saved. Despite all these efforts, Ziegler went into insolvency later that year. It was a sad moment for the family-run business with its proud heritage and dealt a serious blow to many of the staff, including Jochen Brachert, the head of the works council. Downsizing became inevitable and the entire

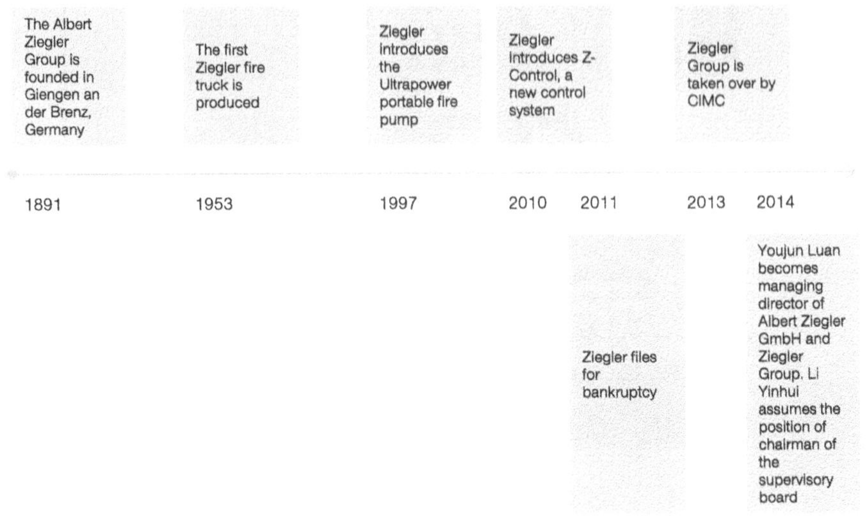

Fig. 7.3 Milestones of Albert Ziegler Group (1891–2014). Source: Ziegler Group

workforce was threatened with losing their jobs. In the end, 150 employees were let go. The fine was just the last straw that broke the camel's back and by no means the only reason for the company's demise. Signs of mismanagement were apparent long before the cartel scandal. The fourth generation of the founding family had been reluctant to invest in the business—buildings were very old; equipment was out of date. In retrospect, it was good for everyone to find a new owner that was willing to invest in the brand and in the people (see Fig. 7.3 for milestones of Albert Ziegler Group).

7.2 Motivation and Strategy

In 2011, the insolvency administrators, Messrs. Kübler, and Sorg took over management of Ziegler, making introduction of proper legal compliance measures as their top priority. The search for potential buyers began immediately and external consultants were soon brought in as interim managers in order to get the business up and running again, while the restructuring program was ongoing. Finding a decent investor was not easy, as it was not certain that Ziegler could ever recover from its damaged reputation. Moreover, in the interest of the local employees, the insolvency administrators were reluctant to sell Ziegler to private equity firms, who would be prone to make a profitable exit in as short a timeframe as possible, jeopardizing Ziegler's future viability.

2012 went by without landing a passable investor, although numerous potential candidates had been screened and interviewed. According to Mr. Kübler's own account, more than 150 companies considered buying Ziegler, but without a result.

Prior to CIMC, another Chinese company, Shandong Heavy Industry, had also shown interest but did not follow through with the deal for reasons unknown.

It was not until March 2013 that CIMC learned about the sale of the insolvent Ziegler Group. It seemed like a sensible investment for CIMC, as Ziegler would complement the product portfolio of CIMC's airport facilities business. Thanks to the ongoing restructuring program, Ziegler was in much better shape than at the beginning of the insolvency procedure. Its production facilities had been upgraded with new equipment and investments had been made in bringing out innovative products, such as the "Merkur", a new type of tunnel rescue vehicle with double cabins, and the "Fire Ant", a special tank fire truck designed for narrow passages. Most importantly, entry orders were picking up again after several large contracts were secured with key accounts, including the State of Hessen and the German Armed Forces. In the third quarter of 2013, Ziegler was even able to regain its position as market leader in Germany, achieving order numbers that it had not seen in a decade.

After the initial discussion, CIMC commissioned due diligence in August 2013 and made it through to the final round of bidding with only another potential buyer, Swiss equipment manufacturer Aebi Schmidt. Ultimately, CIMC outbid its opponent and became the new owner of the Ziegler Group. It turned to be a great result for many stakeholders involved, particularly the employees, as CIMC guaranteed that all employment contracts in Giengen would be kept. As CIMC had an existing business that was complimentary with that of Ziegler, the local communities felt reassured that CIMC meant to develop the Ziegler brand and potentially position it as a global name, building on its decades of experience in international acquisitions and broad customer network in related businesses.

The big day finally arrived on November 7, 2013, when CIMC inked the agreement to acquire Ziegler for 55 million euros, or 1.3 times its net asset value per the end of 2012. The blackout period lasted for 1 month following the signing of the agreement. Li Yinhui, head of CIMC's airport facilities business, took on the post of CEO for the newly-acquired German subsidiary company. It was rather unconventional for a high-ranking executive like Li to assume such a role. Knowing that he would not be managing the Ziegler group on a daily basis, Li asked his deputy Youjun Luan, to oversee Ziegler as acting CEO (or "prokurist" in German) on his behalf. Soon after, Luan was officially appointed CEO to succeed Li, who moved to the supervisory board to serve as chairman.

Ziegler was able to stage a remarkable turnaround within 3 years of the CIMC takeover and was in the black again in 2016. When asked whether there was a master plan for the acquisition, Luan frankly acknowledged that there had been no such a plan at the outset. That said, the purchase formed a clear part of its strategy—CIMC had already been pursuing a diversification strategy and had been looking for attractive investment opportunities around the world for some time. In this regard, the acquisition of Ziegler made perfect sense. According to CIMC's strategy, the airport facilities business unit was going to be one of the main growth drivers for the Chinese conglomerate. Ziegler's airport rescue and firefighting vehicles would enrich the existing product portfolio. Moreover, CIMC's leadership became aware that by building on Ziegler's experience, it could enter the firefighting industry—a completely new market with great growth potential—for the first time.

Europe, the United States, and China are the three biggest markets for firefighting and rescue equipment. Unlike the two Western markets, the Chinese market is highly fragmented. The country's fire truck industry began at the start of twentieth century when all firefighting vehicles were imported from Western countries. In the 1930s, Chinese manufacturers started producing firefighting vehicles locally. Most of them were small to medium-sized companies with outdated technology and weak R&D capabilities. The 1940s and 1950s saw the reorganization and consolidation of the industry, however, to date, no national player really exists.

There were estimated to be around 30,000 firefighting vehicles in service in China in 2014. Annual sales totaled approximately 4000, the majority of which were in the price-sensitive segment served by local players. Compared to developed economies, China was lagging far behind in deploying high-end firefighting and rescue vehicles for special purposes. With the advance of urbanization, the number of high-rise buildings and the complexity of firefighting operations are both expected to rise. Consequently, demand for premium equipment is also on a growth trajectory. CIMC could have a unique competitive advantage with Ziegler under its umbrella, as German brands typically enjoy a good reputation in China and could help CIMC break into new markets.

7.3 Integration and Transformation

By the time of the acquisition, Ziegler had recovered considerably under the management of the insolvency administrators. Nevertheless, challenges abounded when CIMC acquired Ziegler at the end of 2013.

From the experience it had gained during the previous decades, CIMC's leadership knew that there was no panacea for integrating and transforming new subsidiaries. Instead, its success was to be founded on three key pillars: people, organization, and culture. In the case of Ziegler, corporate governance was deficient by any standard. During the insolvency procedure, external consultants with short tenures held most managerial positions. Consequently, CIMC had to rebuild the management team from the ground up after the takeover. Control systems were week within the company that had been family-run for over a century. Business units in different locations used different formats to write books and data quality varied widely. Steering the company remotely from China was clearly not an option.

Li, head of Airport Facilities, was accountable for the Ziegler Group, as Ziegler belonged to his business unit. In a break with convention, Li actually became the first CEO of the revitalized Ziegler Group—a move that signaled Ziegler's importance to CIMC. His long-time deputy, Luan, came on board in November 2013. After a short Christmas and New Year break, he returned to Giengen, accompanied by Leo Deng, a CIMC manager with a background in finance and management systems. They had the mission to revive the ailing German brand on behalf of the Chinese investor.

To the best of our knowledge, this was the first instance in recent years that a Chinese investor had ever appointed a Chinese national as a general manager for a newly-acquired entity in Germany. As a matter of fact, Ziegler was a unique case in that there was essentially no incumbent management. Although Luan kept a low profile at Ziegler, it must have been a daunting task for a Chinese manager to run a German company, which previously had little connection to Chinese business practices or culture. The setup was something quite out of the ordinary for a traditional company rooted in Swabia.

The burning issue that Luan had to resolve first was Ziegler's management team, as the company had been run by lawyers and consultants in the transition period before the takeover. He had to put together a competent team as quickly as possible to bring the business back on its feet. Luan took immediate actions to replace the interim managers with external hires. Nevertheless, the management reshuffle could only take place gradually, as it was practically impossible to find the right people all at once, not to mention that Giengen's location was far from attractive. Even some of the newly hired executives admitted that the company's location was a real concern for them to join Ziegler, although Giengen houses, in fact, at least two other world-famous brands, Bosch and Steiff (the teddy-bear maker). It took some time to make these adjustments, but the reshuffle is now complete. Before the insolvency, there was practically no board of management as the Ziegler family effectively made all decisions. Soon after CIMC's ownership began, a brand-new board of management was appointed, headed by Luan. It was a highly international and diversified team, consisting of six people from four countries, China, Germany, the Netherlands, and Croatia. Luan was the only Chinese national on the board. However, the real innovative bit was the rotation mechanism. Two of the six seats on the board are up for re-selection by the standing members of the board every 2 years. The board member candidates are experienced managers within the Ziegler Group that have demonstrated exemplary performances. This mechanism was introduced as a way to reward and incentivize top performers. In addition to the board of management, a supervisory board was formed to steer the strategic direction of the company.

In its entire history, the Ziegler Group had been a highly decentralized organization. Its satellite factories were highly independent, somewhat resembling franchises. Decision-making procedures were not formalized and synergy potential was largely untapped, while there was an abundance of overlapping organizational functions between the headquarters and the subsidiaries. After taking over leadership, Luan initiated the centralization of group functions. For example, payroll administration, the appointment of personnel, procurement, marketing, and sales at all Ziegler's subsidiaries were unified. Group-wide rules were developed and implemented across Ziegler to reinforce the headquarters' central role in functional management. The integration of HR, IT, finance, procurement, and R&D is now completed and group directors for these functions have taken up their positions. The management optimization process is set to continue at a subsidiary level in the coming years according to Luan's plan.

In the meantime, the new management took on the internal auditing and management control systems of the subsidiaries. According to CIMC's policy, a complete compliance package should consist of financial books, corporate governance, business administration, duty incompatibility, and related-party transactions, etc. The old Ziegler group was plagued by a multitude of compliance issues and although legal compliance improved considerably during the insolvency period, it still was below international standards. Specifically, the scope of non-legal compliance at Ziegler was narrow, only taking into account sales and marketing, procurement, and employee ethics. The starting situation at Ziegler was far from satisfactory. For example, the financial books from different subsidiaries were neither standardized nor compliant with German accounting standards (Generally Accepted Accounting Standards). It is easy to imagine how difficult it was for the managers to run the business. A comprehensive analysis was conducted and improvement plans were devised. After a couple of years, the majority of the issues with management control systems had been resolved, and booking had been unified to a large extent. Every factory was required to submit financial books to the headquarters on a monthly basis. The gap to CIMC's own standards of risk management and control systems had narrowed significantly.

At a traditional Swabian company, like Ziegler, employees play an important role and can exert considerable influence on managerial decisions. Most employees were members of IG Metall (Industrial Union of Metalworkers), the largest and the most influential workers' union in Europe. Its name does not do it justice as it represents the interests of not only employees in the mining of minerals but also those in many other different industries. If relations with the employees were not handled appropriately, it could have had severe repercussions for CIMC and any future M&A's it wished to undertake in Europe. For this reason, immediately assuming office, Luan began collaborating closely with the works council and tried to have open discussions with the employees. CIMC leadership sent a very clear message to all staff at the first employee communication meeting, reaffirming CIMC's promise to keep every job at Giengen and further develop the Ziegler brand.

This was a big promise but CIMC kept its word. Not only were the existing jobs secured, many new jobs were also created, at the headquarters in Giengen and other locations inside and outside Germany (see Fig. 7.4). The number of employees in Germany rose from 699 in 2013 to 861 in 2016, while the total workforce grew from 1079 to 1330 in the same period, representing a 23% increase. Recruiting and developing new talent has become a top priority at Ziegler. New employees are teamed with experienced staff to learn from their experience and best practices. Under the new human resources structure, recently hired personnel have to attend mandatory training sessions with newly developed curricula. With the planned expansion of production sites, even more staff are expected to be hired in the coming years.

Collaboration with the works council went smoothly. The head of the works council, Jochen Brachert, who also recently became a member of the supervisory board, recalls that he did not have any preconceived notions about the Chinese investors prior to the takeover. Even in worst case, it could only be better than the insolvency. Looking back at the last 3 years, he is pleased with the progress thus far. He and the works council have had meetings with Luan every 2 weeks to address the

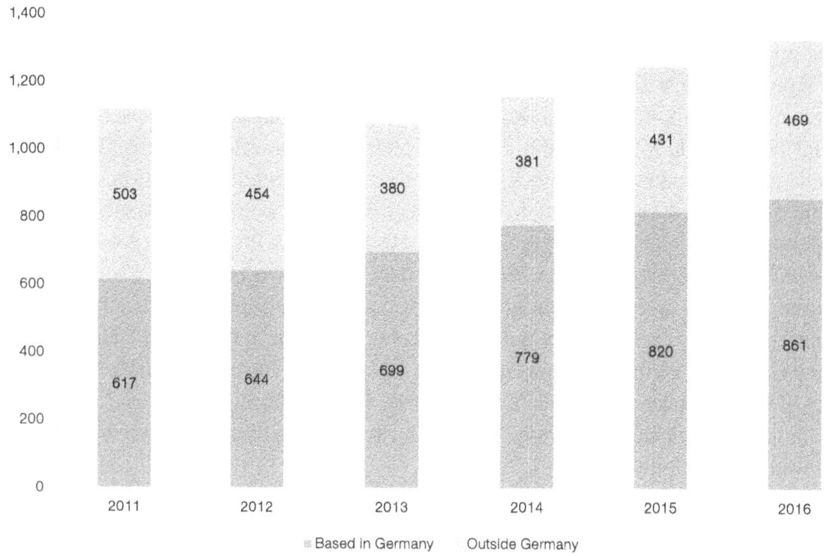

Fig. 7.4 Number of employees at Ziegler (2011–2016). Source: Ziegler Group

workers' concerns. In addition, he and Luan go to the shop floor on a regular basis to talk to the workers directly. The staff members appreciated the respect they were shown and that they were attentively listened to—something that cannot be taken for granted in large organizations in Germany. Brachert valued Luan's openness and sincerity in handling staff-related issues. Moreover, from his conversations with his colleagues at IG Metall, he learned that Chinese investors at other German companies had exercised similar care to keep jobs and treat employees fairly.

Luan and Deng decided that their role should be to act as bridges, giving guidance and facilitating communication between Ziegler and the holding company, rather than merely supervising. In any case, the prerequisite for their role was mutual understanding. The Chinese managers could not speak German and their German counterparts could not speak Chinese. They had to resort to English as the lingua franca. Although Ziegler had an international customer base and subsidiaries in remote countries, the local German staff were not fluent in English. It took several years for the organization to adapt to its new company speak. Now all management meetings are held and documented in English. Nevertheless, German remains as the dominant language on the shop floor among technicians and assembly workers. To accommodate Brachert, the workers' representative on the supervisory board, a German-speaking Chinese colleague would interpret for him during important meetings. It had been a difficult change for everyone, but Luan firmly and fully implemented the new language requirement. During our interviews with the members of the board, they joked that, thanks to Luan's policy, they all speak better English by now. The management team also adopted WeChat, a popular instant communication app from China, as a communication tool among themselves. René

Pol, Group CSO at Ziegler, even could show off by using a hidden feature imbedded in the app that translates chats from Chinese into English instantly.

Gaining the trust of the workforce and the management team was an important achievement for the Chinese investor in the post-M&A integration phase. The next crucial task was to win over the customer base and grow the business. The cartel scandal and the ensuing insolvency had left a mark on Ziegler's reputation. Although this recovered to a certain extent during the insolvency period, customers' trust in Ziegler remained vulnerable. Having a Chinese investor with a strong governmental connection did not do much to help, especially considering many of Ziegler's key accounts had ties to the German government or military. While Li was still CEO at Ziegler, reassuring the company's main customers was top of his agenda. He traveled around Germany, visiting the most important customers, in an effort to dispel concerns over CIMC's connection with the Chinese state. His approach worked, as Ziegler was able to maintain the German Armed Forces as one of its customers and win new orders in the subsequent years.

Under Luan's stewardship, Ziegler was able to achieve steady revenue growth year after year. 2016 stood out in particular, with revenue soaring to 220 million euros, representing a 26% year-on-year growth (see Fig. 7.5). In contrast, the industry's average growth rate has been declining for years and was estimated to be just 1.6% in the same time period.

In 2016, Ziegler finally returned to the profit zone, booking a positive EBIT of nearly 5 million euros, or 2.1% in relative terms (see Fig. 7.6). It was the first time in at least 5 years that the Ziegler Group as a whole was profitable again.

This success was the result of improvements on multiple fronts, in addition to those previously mentioned regarding compliance and management control systems. To start with, CIMC attached great importance to R&D. After taking over Ziegler, it continuously expanded the R&D team in Germany and increased spending on new

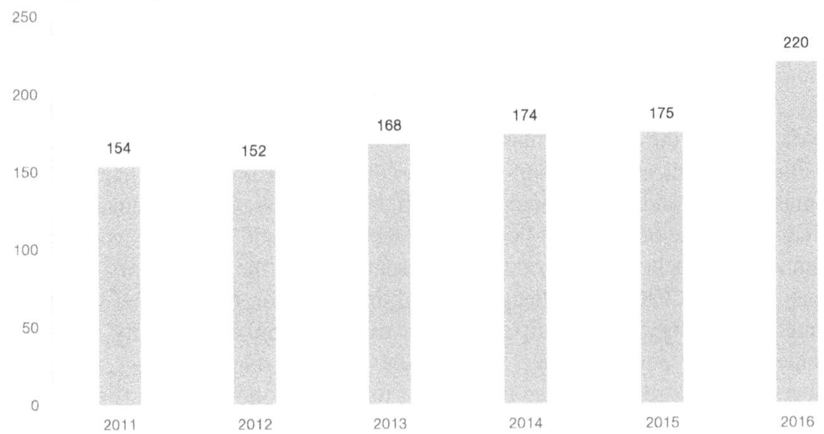

Fig. 7.5 Revenue of Ziegler Group (2011–2016). Source: Ziegler Group

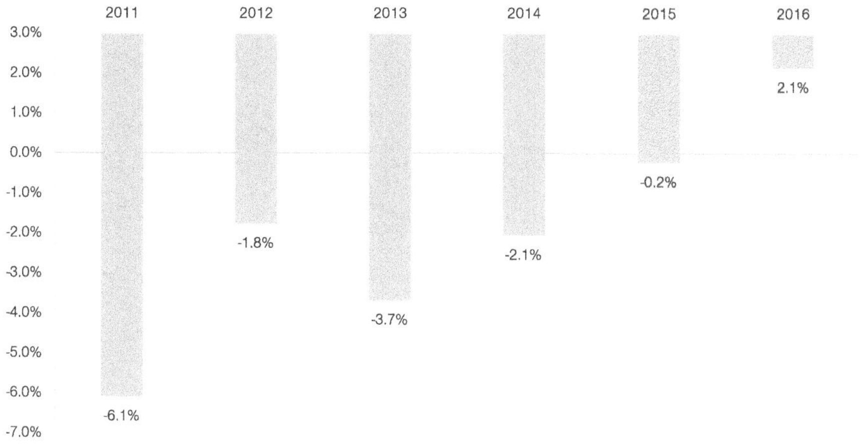

Fig. 7.6 EBIT margin of Ziegler Group (2011–2016). Source: Ziegler Group

product development. Since CIMC's acquisition, the size of the R&D team at Ziegler has grown by 50%. In the same period, expenditure as a percentage of revenue has doubled to 3.2% (see Fig. 7.7). On average, hidden champions spend 6% of their revenue on R&D. According to this benchmark, Ziegler still has room for improvement.

That being said, the investment Ziegler has made so far has already borne fruit. Ziegler managed to file 19 patents in 2016 alone, an improvement of nearly 100% compared to before the insolvency (see Fig. 7.8). Product innovations have been well received, such as the Alpas (Aluminum-Panel-System) III; the next-generation airport rescue vehicle Z-Class 2020; the spacious truck cabin Z-Cab NG XL; and an upgrade of the control unit Z-Control 2.0. Some of these projects have already delivered finished products that have been sold to customers, while others are still under development but are on schedule.

From 2014 onward, the revenue contribution of new products rose dramatically, from zero prior to 2014 to 75 million euros in 2016, i.e. more than 55% of annual revenue. Innovation clearly became Ziegler's growth engine, laying a good foundation for sustainable top-line growth (Fig. 7.9).

Innovation did not only apply to the products but also the production facilities. Contrary to its image as a technology-driven company, the Giengen plant had been reliant on outdated manufacturing processes and had more in common with manual workshops. The layout of the shop floor was suboptimal, causing inefficiency in production. In an effort to modernize the plant, the new Ziegler management team drew up a strategy for production and logistics, focusing on optimizing floor layout and assembly procedures. Ziegler had the chance to carry out the optimization of its production processes in parallel to completing a large order for a key account. After the upgrade, Ziegler was able to drastically increase efficiency and reduce lead time. In order to ensure the success of the optimization project, progress was assessed on

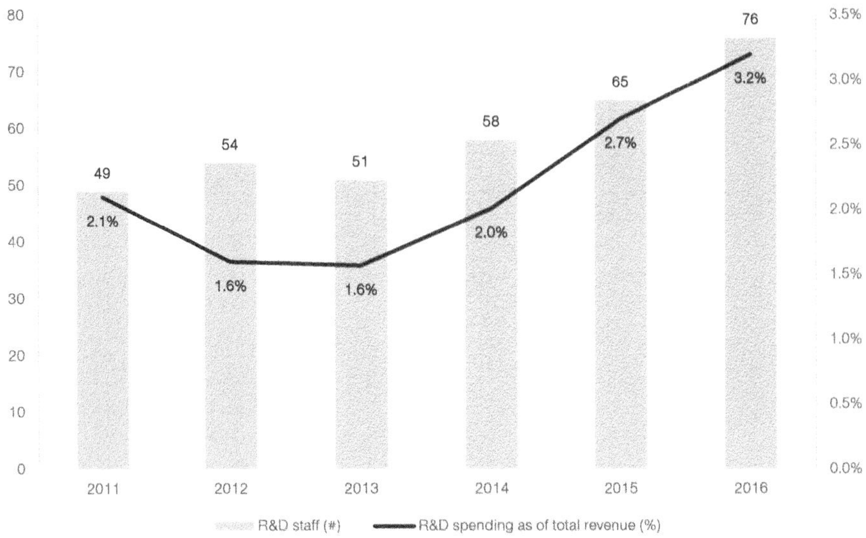

Fig. 7.7 R&D staff and spending at Ziegler (2011–2016). Source: Ziegler Group

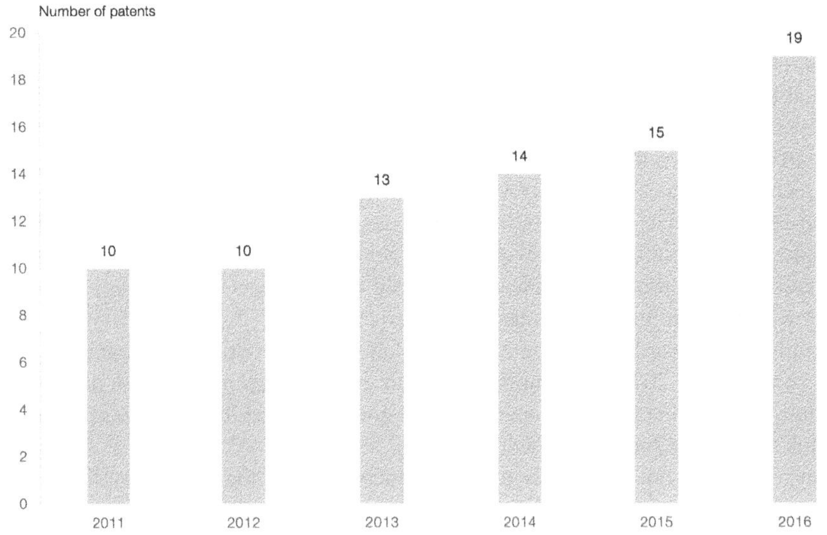

Fig. 7.8 Patents filed by Ziegler (2011–2016). Source: Ziegler Group

set days each week so that potential problems could be dealt with before they became serious issues.

René Pol, a Dutch national, was appointed Group CSO after Ziegler became part of CIMC. He is a veteran at Ziegler Group, having worked for the company on and off since the early 1990s. He noted that Ziegler had been overwhelmingly focused on continental Europe as its target market. International markets were basically ignored,

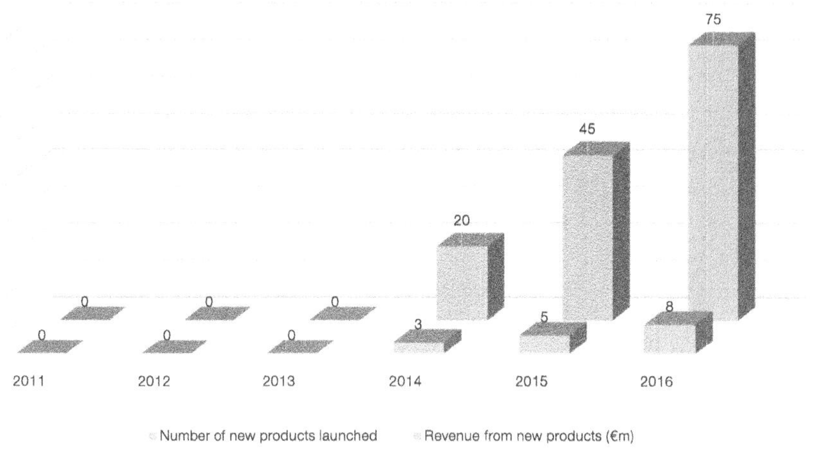

Fig. 7.9 New products and their revenue contribution (2011–2016). Source: Ziegler Group

as the owners did not aspire to make the company a global player. The organizational structure had not been conducive to overseas business as there was no dedicated team to take care of pre-sales consultation or aftersales service for international customers, not to mention that hardly anyone at the headquarters could communicate properly in English. The internationalization of the business has gained momentum under CIMC's ownership. The sales and customer service infrastructure has been revamped, and a dedicated team of sales and support staff has been built to assist international customers. A sales-driven subsidiary of Ziegler, wholly owned by CIMC, was founded in Beijing to be close to local customers and provide more agile services. As of 2016, there were about a dozen sales and service staff working out of the Beijing subsidiary. CIMC was also instrumental in generating new business opportunities for Ziegler from its broad network of local Chinese customers. A case in point was the order from Guangxi Nanning fire department, which ordered 17 large multi-functional urban fire trucks from Ziegler as early as 2014. It was the first time in Ziegler's history that it delivered fire trucks to a Chinese customer in such a big volume.

CIMC's lead-generation capability stretches beyond China as it has operations in many parts of the world. Ziegler benefitted from the airport facilities business unit in particular as their customers overlapped. Pol mentioned that a few leads had been referred to Ziegler by colleagues in the airport facilities division.

The market-oriented growth strategy paid off evidently. In the past, the company generated over three quarters of its revenue in Germany, according to Pol. While the share of revenue generated in Germany had hovered around 60% in 2013, this proportion dropped to below 50% 3 years later, with China contributing significantly to revenue growth outside Germany (see Fig. 7.10a, b). Revenue contribution from China rose from almost none in 2013 to 12% in 2016, accounting for 70% of revenue from Asia.

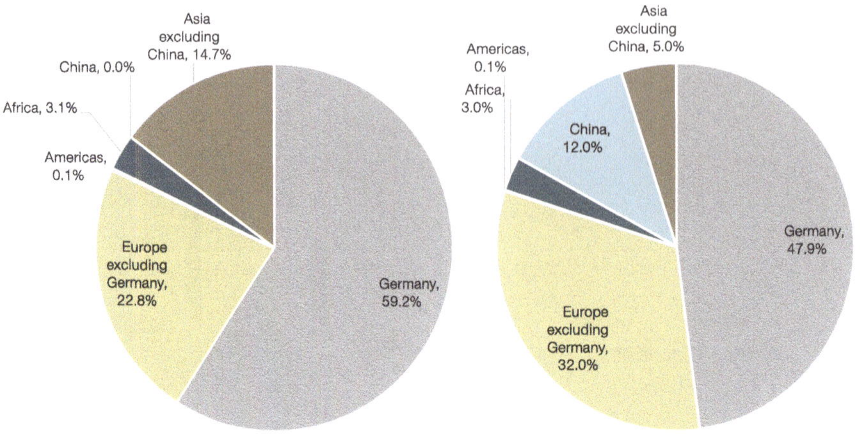

Fig. 7.10 (**a**) Revenue by region (2013). (**b**) Revenue by region (2016). Source: Ziegler Group

A more open, market-oriented Ziegler has taken shape since being acquired by CIMC. Not only has domestic business stabilized and growth picked up, Ziegler has also initiated a course of internationalization. Continuous efforts to innovate and streamline corporate governance laid a solid foundation for the next stage of development under CIMC's leadership.

7.4 Growth Initiatives

The revived Albert Ziegler Group broke even 3 years after becoming part of CIMC and was well positioned for future growth. Within the company, a new corporate-governance set-up had been introduced, providing transparency and efficiency, and a well-functioning, competent management team was now up and running. Externally, the negative impact of the cartel incident and the subsequent insolvency had gradually diminished. Ziegler restored its reputation as a leading manufacturer of quality firefighting and rescue equipment. Prospects looked good for Ziegler, as it began to emerge as a rising global player with comprehensive support from the holding company.

As to where the journey was headed, CIMC/Ziegler had a clear answer. A special task force consisting of members from both CIMC and Ziegler spent more than 6 months together devising "Strategy 2020", a 5-year plan outlining the way forward. The core of the strategy aimed for CIMC to become the world's leading provider of firefighting and rescue solutions. Ziegler, as a premium brand and technological powerhouse, would play a central role in achieving that goal.

Luan explained that by 2020, CIMC's firefighting and rescue business unit would be comprised of a fleet of affiliated companies, among which Ziegler would serve as the flagship, promoting new technologies and sharing critical expertise and best practices with the other members of the unit. By 2020, CIMC/Ziegler aims to have established a prominent presence in all major markets, i.e. Europe, China, and the Americas.

The overall sales plan forecasts an 18% compounded annual growth rate over a 5-year timeframe. Organic growth at Ziegler should average around 10% over the same period. In view of the average industry growth rate, which was in the low single digits, the plan was extremely ambitious. German employees soon voiced their concerns over the challenging target. One of the matters they raised was that quality could suffer as a consequence. To substantiate the growth plan and address the employees' concerns, the task force defined 57 specific projects, spanning a broad range of areas, such as operations, sales, finances, services, supply chain, and IT.

Operative efficiency had improved remarkably at the Giengen plant owing to its proximity to the group's headquarters. Yet progress at other plants varied by a wide margin, as they had been historically managed in isolated silos, meaning there was still room for improvement in general.

Looking ahead, the company's management structure and processes will be further optimized to reduce costs and increase efficiency. Some small or unprofitable entities will be closed if they no longer make economic sense. The roles of each plant within the group will be more clearly defined to tap synergies to the fullest. For example, Giengen, as the headquarters of the Ziegler Group, will be responsible for developing and manufacturing standard vehicles such as the HLF series and Z series. Production capacity in Giengen will expand with the addition of a new service center located 6 km from the headquarters. Capacity in Mühlau will be fully utilized to manufacture different types of standard vehicles, such as the MLF and TSF, while Rendsburg will become an important service hub in addition to producing model series, including the TSF and KLF.

A large proportion of the increased operational efficiency should result from the "Configurator Project", which was launched in 2016. The aim of the project is to streamline the information flow between sales and production teams, and increase the accuracy of costing by using standardized bills of materials. Furthermore, the Configurator should speed up processes, from costing and production preparation to manufacturing standard-specification products, supported by modularized bills of materials and price lists. Upon completion of the project, standard components stored at all production sites will be harmonized, leading to reduced costs and faster production ramp-up through improved availability of spare parts.

In regard to future growth drivers, Luan names two important levers. The first is investing continuously in R&D to secure Ziegler's competitive edge and a premium position within the industry. The second lever is pushing forward the internationalization of the Ziegler Group. The last 10 years of the company is a lost decade. Its biggest competitor, Rosenbauer, used to be about the same size as Ziegler. While Ziegler was content to sit back and reap the benefits of the cartel agreement, Rosenbauer, also a member of the cartel, kept on investing and successfully expanded in the US market. As of now, Rosenbauer's annual revenue is approaching 900 million euros—four times that of Ziegler.

As part of CIMC, Ziegler has the chance to resume its growth path worldwide and narrow the gap to Rosenbauer, especially in China, where CIMC/Ziegler has built a good foundation over the last couple of years. The subsidiary in Beijing will be able to provide consultation and aftersales services at a speed that would have been impossible a few years ago. Ziegler's sister company, CFE has a very strong presence in Sichuan thanks to Sichuan Chuanxiao's sales network and production base. Chuanxiao was founded in 1963 under the name Sichuan Firefighting Equipment General Works, a state-owned enterprise. Since 1995, it has been a 100% subsidiary company of CFE. It is a valuable asset as, the central government no longer issues licenses for manufacturing firefighting vehicles in China. Although there has been little cooperation between Ziegler and Chuanxiao so far, the potential synergy is significant in a variety of areas, such as purchasing, R&D, and more importantly, sales and marketing activities. As a first step, Ziegler recently made plans to seek and develop strategic suppliers in China through its entity in Beijing. In the medium to long term, CIMC aims to be the first national player to gain at least a 30% market share in China.

Although the prospects in China are bright, it will not be an easy win, says Pol, CSO of the Ziegler Group. According to his estimates, the annual market volume for firefighting and rescue vehicles is around 4000 in total, and the addressable market (i.e. high-end, imported vehicles) is only one-tenth of the total market, reducing the market potential for Ziegler to 400. Ziegler delivered about 100 fire trucks to China in 2015. The room for significant growth could be limited unless the overall market size increases or demand shifts toward more high-end products. Another practical hurdle for foreign companies in general is the so-called 3C inspection imposed on all fire vehicles before they can be handed over to end users. Such inspections can only be carried out in China, resulting in additional costs and extended delivery time for foreign manufacturers. It is common practice across the world.

To counter these entry barriers, CIMC/Ziegler is evaluating alternative business models. One option would be to adopt a model similar to the one employed by Apple. This would mean products would be designed by Ziegler in Germany, while the necessary local modifications and assembly would take place at production sites close to where the orders are made, be they in China, South Africa, or anywhere else. This solution would also alleviate the capacity bottleneck at Ziegler's European plants, which has already forced Ziegler to turn down valuable orders and pay penalties for delayed deliveries.

In 2016, the first year under "Strategy 2020", Ziegler achieved 220 million euros in revenue, beating its original target by 6%. Various improvement projects are currently underway, paving the way for it to become a world leader in firefighting and rescue solutions.

7.5 Closing Remarks

The contrast in the Ziegler case was intriguing as the acquiring company, CIMC, was a heavyweight industrial conglomerate with a strong governmental background and an international outlook, while the acquired company, Ziegler, was a small family-run business rooted in the Swabian Alb area, a region usually known for its conservatism. How did they come together? How did they get along with each other? What challenges did they face? Where will their journey lead?

The situation is quite unlike the typical acquisition one would expect from a Chinese investor. In recent years, Chinese investors have tended to apply the "partnering approach" to the post-M&A integration phase. The core belief underpinning the strategy is that the incumbent management possesses market knowledge and relationships that are key to the success of the acquired company. As such, the senior managers should be retained after the acquisition. The Chinese investor has more to gain by partnering with them and interfering as little as possible. Obviously, CIMC did not have the privilege of a competent incumbent management team when it closed the deal. It was Luan, CEO of the Ziegler Group, who almost single-handedly built a new management team and reinstated corporate governance at the formerly family-run business. His approach succeeded—business turned around in just 3 years and Ziegler expects to stay profitable for years to come. Although he modestly describes his role as acting as a bridge between Ziegler and CIMC, there was clearly more to this success story. Overcoming cultural differences was only the tip of the iceberg—there were a plethora of challenges. This case study has probably discussed only a small number of these.

As the title of the case study suggests, the firefighting and rescue sector is a new area of business for CIMC. Entry into this sector was mostly down to good fortune, as there was initially no plan to develop firefighting and rescue equipment as a core business. Ziegler came to CIMC's attention because it was thought that it would complement its airport facilities business. The potential of Ziegler's own business area was only realized later. It is worth noting how quickly CIMC adapted its strategy toward Ziegler, navigating unchartered waters with a series of special measures.

Probably the most interesting aspect of the CIMC/Ziegler case is whether the company will indeed succeed in becoming a prominent global player in the firefighting and rescue equipment business. CIMC achieved this feat once before with its container business many years ago. Now, it is better positioned and has many more resources at its disposal. Does this mean that its odds of succeeding have improved?

In any case, CIMC will not limit itself to organic growth but continue to engage in M&A's of firefighting-related companies in the coming years, filling the gaps in its geographic and product portfolios. As a matter of fact, at the time of writing, CIMC/Ziegler had just acquired a minority stake in CELA S. r. L., a private Italian company and a hidden champion, specializing in industrial working platforms, firefighting platforms, and water towers. In 2016, the company's revenue was 18 million euros. Through equity participation, Ziegler was able to gain strategic access to a key firefighting-related technology, allowing it to provide better custom-made solutions for customers in need of elevated work platforms and water towers.

The voyage of the revived Ziegler Group under the umbrella of CIMC has just started. New shores await ahead.

Part III

Expert Interviews

Interview with Dr. Sun Shaojun, Executive President of Weichai Power Co., Ltd

8

This interview was conducted on July 27th 2017 and was published with kind permission of Dr. Sun Shaojun.

Sun Shaojun is the executive president of Weichai Power Co. Ltd. and chairman of the advisory board at Linde Hydraulics GmbH & Co. KG.

8.1 About Weichai Power Co., Ltd

Founded in 2002 in Weifang, China, Weichai Power Co., Ltd. staged its initial public offering (IPO) on the Hong Kong Stock Exchange in 2004 and later re-listed in mainland China in 2007, which was something that had never been done before. By concentrating on industrial operations and strategic investments, Weichai Power has successfully built four complementary business units: powertrain (including engine, transmission, and axles), vehicles and engines, hydraulics, and spare parts. The company also possesses core technologies to produce construction machinery. Weichai Power is widely recognized as one of the leading Chinese automotive and industrial equipment manufacturers, providing comprehensive and competitive solutions to its customers.

As a one of the first Chinese enterprises to venture abroad, Weichai Power's overseas business includes subsidiaries across the world, such as Kion (Germany), Linde Hydraulics (Germany), Moteurs Baudouin (France), and Ferretti (Italy) in Europe, as well as Power Solutions International, a manufacturer of clean engines and power systems, and Dematic, a supply chain automation specialist based in the United States. Moreover, Weichai Power has a strategic outlook for Asia in line with the Chinese government's "One Belt One Road" policy. For example, 20% of the engines supplied to the biggest Iranian bus manufacturer are made by Weichai Power. Other regions, such as Southeast Asia, Russia, the Middle East, and Africa have also traditionally been important OEM markets for Weichai Power. Today, all

J. Y. Yang et al., *Chinese M&As in Germany*, Management for Professionals,
https://doi.org/10.1007/978-3-319-99405-5_8

of its overseas subsidiary companies make a profit, generating approximately half of Weichai Power's annual revenue, which is approaching 100 billion yuan.

Authors What are the driving forces behind Weichai Power's M&A activities overseas, particularly in Germany?

Sun We are in constant pursuit of strategic assets that will enable us to fill the gaps in our product portfolio and develop our core competencies. Take our powertrain business unit, for example: Weichai Power boasts a complete product line from engines through transmission to axles for heavy-duty vehicles. Offering the full range of products not only allows us to provide our customers with comprehensive solutions, it also enhances our overall competitive advantage.

The logic behind acquiring Kion and Linde Hydraulics was that it would enable Weichai to build a comprehensive product line. Hydraulic technologies are so crucial to construction machinery that there is a saying: "Whoever controls hydraulic components trumps the industry." Hydraulics have a direct impact on safety issues and are often considered the main indicator of a nation's competitiveness in the field of machinery and equipment manufacturing. Although China is progressing at a fast pace in this industry, high-end hydraulic technologies have traditionally been held by a small number of companies, such as Bosch (Germany), Kawasaki (Japan), and Eaton (USA). Lacking these core technologies, Chinese companies have to rely entirely on imported hydraulic systems to manufacture pump trucks, excavators, loaders, and forklifts, etc., which goes against China's domestic strategy of upgrading our infrastructure and obtaining key technologies. One of the most efficient ways for a company to obtain the technologies it needs is through mergers and acquisitions. After the preliminary evaluation of several leading hydraulic systems manufacturers, we quickly narrowed down our targets to Linde Hydraulics in the Kion Group.

By integrating Moteurs Baudouin, Ferretti, Dematic, Kion, and Linde Hydraulics, establishing manufacturing plants in India and Belarus, and transferring technologies to Myanmar and Ethiopia, Weichai Power has successfully implemented its preliminary global strategic layout. Currently, all of these subsidiary companies are making a profit and our overseas business contributes approximately half of Weichai Power's annual revenue. As a result, we will continue to look for suitable investment targets internationally, including potential M&As.

Authors What impact will China's restrictions on outbound investments have on M&A activities in Germany in the future? Will lawmakers in Europe increase their scrutiny of future M&A deals? Will restrictive policies become a long-term trend?

Sun I am not worried at all. On the contrary, I actually believe government intervention makes sense. In terms of Weichai Power, restrictive policies do not have much of an impact. Weichai Power only acquires industrial companies in order to expand our core competencies, which are in line with our domestic strategy. In addition, all of our target companies overseas are from non-sensitive sectors. Therefore, we will not face significant pushback from governments in host regions.

Authors What challenges did Weichai Power face when integrating Linde Hydraulics and how did Weichai Power overcome them?

Sun Minimizing the impact of misunderstandings and cultural differences is the most important challenge. Ensuring all sides communicate frequently and effectively is an essential success factor. For instance, Germans are known for making plans and then sticking to them, while the Chinese tend to be flexible and sometimes even challenge the rules that are already in place. It can seem as though the German and Chinese corporate cultures are at the two opposite ends of the spectrum.

As soon as I came to Linde Hydraulics in January 2013, I spoke to more than 20 key employees and explained to them that Weichai Power is a strategic investor. I always clarify three things to the Linde Hydraulics workforce at the annual employee meeting: Weichai Power's goals and growth strategy; upcoming collaboration work between Weichai Power and Linde Hydraulics as well as our expected outcomes; and finally, that Weichai Power fully supports the long-term development of Linde Hydraulics.

Weichai Power's investment is beneficial for the growth of Linde Hydraulics. This is not only a slogan, it is also a fact. After being carved out from Kion Group, Linde Hydraulics received an additional investment of 58 million euros from Weichai Power to build a new plant in Aschaffenburg, which went into operation in July 2016. Weichai Power has proved that growing Linde Hydraulics is in the interest of everyone involved.

To reinforce organizational cohesion, we also organized so-called "Family Day", inviting more than 1000 employees and their families to visit the company. The modern working environment impressed them very much, which improved the Chinese investor's image and enhanced the workforce's sense of belonging and pride in Weichai Power. We also organized soccer tournaments with mixed teams of Chinese and German staff, breaking down stereotypic psychological barriers between the two nationalities.

Authors Could you shed some light on Weichai Power's management approach for Linde Hydraulics after the acquisition?

Sun Generally speaking, Chinese investors tend to apply one of three approaches to managing their acquired foreign entities:

- The investor controls the finances but does not get involved in operations
- The investor replaces all existing executives with staff from the parent company (a typical approach used by US investors)
- The investor participates strategically in management by steering the growth strategy of the acquired firm while identifying and resolving issues through a well-designed key performance indicator (KPI) system

Weichai Power adopted the third approach in managing Linde Hydraulics. The executive positions are filled by German employees, who are responsible for daily business but also play an important role in defining growth strategies for Linde Hydraulics.

It is very common for German companies to have a dual-board system as their corporate structure, consisting of a management board and a supervisory board. The Linde Hydraulics management board is made up of senior managers and is in charge of daily operations. It holds a weekly meeting and books to the supervisory board, which is made up of shareholder and employee representatives. It meets once a quarter and its responsibilities include appointing and overseeing the members of the management board as well as being involved in important decision-making processes. In order to identify and address issues promptly, we also set up an advisory board made up of representatives of the two major shareholders, Weichai Power and Kion. By holding monthly meetings, the advisory board greatly improves the efficacy and efficiency of decision-making. I serve as the chairman of the advisory board and also sit on the supervisory board.

Weichai Power has seconded approximately 50 employees to Aschaffenburg overall since the acquisition. Currently, 15 Weichai Power employees work in various departments at Linde Hydraulics, such as finance, legal, engineering, and marketing, as we speak. The colleagues in the finance and legal departments are responsible for helping Chinese shareholders perform effective management control functions, while the main task of the colleagues in the R&D, engineering, and marketing departments is to learn from Linde Hydraulics' management experience and study its advanced technologies and management know-hows. When they repatriate, we make sure that they will be playing the first fiddle in their own team, no matter how big it is. Only this way they can practice what they have learned to the full.

At the same time, German engineers from Linde Hydraulics have also have the chance to transfer to Weichai Power's headquarters in China. This bilateral exchange improves understanding and trust between Chinese and German employees in an efficient way.

Authors Has Weichai Power introduced incentive systems at Linde Hydraulics like those that are commonly seen in China?

Sun It is just not realistic to export Chinese incentive systems to Germany wholesale, even if we like to. For instance, German salespeople consider selling to be their job and do not expect extra compensation for good performance, therefore their salary is basically fixed. In China, the income of sales staff depends heavily on their sales performance. Any attempt to restructure the compensation packages of German salespeople would face major pushback and require approval from the works council.

On the other hand, German salespeople would value much more non-financial incentives. Every year, we honor the sales staff with the best performances. This recognition is greatly appreciated by the winners. For example, I took the winners out to dinner at the end of last year. The following day, everyone in the company already knew about it: "Mr. Sun from Weichai Power invited me to dinner!" Such personal recognition is a great honor for German employees.

Authors Weichai Power uses a "light" management style at Linde Hydraulics and gives the German team considerable latitude to run the firm in a German way. Has Weichai Power considered changing the current approach and strengthening the role of the Chinese managers in coming years as they accumulate experience in overseas management?

Sun Why should we? We are very satisfied with the current approach, which the last few years have shown to be pragmatic and effective, but we do differentiate our approaches at different acquired entities. For instance, because of the business overlap between Weichai Power and our newly acquired company PSI, huge synergy potential is expected. After the acquisition, we set up a coordination committee, which is in charge of integration and harnessing synergy, and various coordination task forces that book to the committee. Furthermore, we sent a representative of the Chinese shareholders (vice-president level) to join the management. Weichai Power does not have a universal approach to running foreign subsidiaries. In our opinion, there is no single best solution. It is essential that the adopted management approach fits the specific situation.

Authors How do you view the role the works council played before the acquisition as well as during the integration phase? What is your take on the cooperation between the works council and Chinese investors?

Sun Unlike works councils in China, German works councils are so powerful that they have an impact on corporate operations and management. Similar to our approach for the management team, we strive to maintain transparent and effective communication with the works council. I have monthly meetings with the chairperson of the council at Linde Hydraulics. We respect each other and share the same goal—a better future for the company. Once we find this common ground, it is relatively easy to find solutions to other problems. For example, earlier this year, there was a period during which we received too many orders and were not able to process them on time. After consulting the works councils, the workforce agreed to work on the weekends to catch up with the orders. Under the previous circumstances, where there was no trust between the employers and employees, this would have been simply impossible.

To promote bilateral communication and understanding, we invited representatives of Linde Hydraulics' works council to Weichai Power's headquarters in China to learn more about how the Chinese works union operates. Likewise, we invited representatives of our Chinese works council to visit their counterparts in Germany.

Authors According to our experience, German R&D teams are highly competent overall, however, the projects tend to progress at a relatively slow pace. Has Weichai Power any insights on how to address this issue?

Sun This is a common phenomenon, which we have encountered at Linde Hydraulics as well. The German technicians have rigid working times, usually 37 h a week. Overtime should be compensated and therefore it is generally not encouraged by the management. It is also worth noting that the German technicians have a good work ethic and a strong sense of responsibility. If there is an urgent situation, they are willing to work overtime as required. To expedite and improve the research projects, we chose to form a team made up of both German and Chinese technicians. In some cases, the German technicians take charge of the early phase, while Chinese engineers carry out the later phase in China. In other instances, the Chinese technicians come to Aschaffenburg to work alongside their German colleagues, enabling us to better manage the project progress, as Chinese engineers are often more flexible regarding working hours.

Authors Can you talk about how Weichai Power enables internal knowledge management and learning?

Sun First, we rely on in-depth learning. For example we send Chinese employees to Germany to work in the corresponding department for a period of time, and when they return to China, they share the knowledge and experience they acquired in Germany with their other Chinese colleagues. Experience working overseas also facilitates communication with foreign colleagues. Linde Hydraulics is particularly proficient at quality management, which is why we send our employees to learn from their experience in this area.

In addition, joint projects are highly conducive to knowledge sharing as we have seen how well working together facilitates communication and learning.

Authors How can the research competency of a German company and the marketing competency of a Chinese company be combined effectively?

Sun These are essentially two distinct kinds of corporate values. If any company could achieve this combination it would be invincible, so obviously it is not an easy task.

On the whole, Chinese companies are highly sensitive to market dynamics and strive to respond to the market in a timely fashion in order to maintain or increase their market share. In contrast, German companies are mostly technology-driven and tend to focus on improving the quality of the product but are not sufficiently sensitive to the market. I have spent a lot time talking to our German colleagues, including the head of R&D. However good the products' quality might be, what good does it do if it cannot be sold? Weichai Power believes customer satisfaction comes first and will offer our customers whatever they need. Gradually, our German colleagues began to see the merit of our thinking and started paying greater attention to customers' requirements. Meanwhile, their existing technological advantages are still their core competitive advantage. For this reason, our current strategy for Linde Hydraulics combines the strength of both sides and is referred to as the "market-driven approach based on product leadership".

Authors Thank you for sharing with us and we wish Weichai Power a bright future.

9 Interview with Mr. Wang Wei, a Partner Specializing in Transaction Services at PwC Germany

This interview was conducted on August 9th 2017 and was published with kind permission of Mr. Wang Wei.

Wang Wei is a seasoned expert in Sino-German M&As. He serves as the only representative from any of the Big Four accounting firms to sit on the nomination committee for the CHKD Invest Award, a prize conferred by the Chinese Chamber of Commerce in Germany and sponsored by the Chinese Ministry of Commerce.

9.1 About PwC Germany

PwC is one of the Big Four accounting firms worldwide. With over 10,000 employees and revenue of nearly 1.9 billion euros in 2016, PwC Germany is the biggest auditing and accounting firm in the country.

Authors What factors drive Chinese companies to go overseas for M&As? Have these factors changed from a decade ago?

Wang At that time, the main driver of Chinese overseas M&As was securing access to natural resources and technology. In recent years, the motives for business mergers have become more diversified. In general, market strategy and globalization are being afforded ever greater importance. For private enterprises, asset allocation is not the main driver of their investments in German companies. It is also rare for state-owned enterprises to invest solely in order to expand.

Authors Why is Germany so attractive to Chinese companies? What will be the trending industries for investment in Germany in the next few years?

J. Y. Yang et al., *Chinese M&As in Germany*, Management for Professionals,
https://doi.org/10.1007/978-3-319-99405-5_9

Wang About 500–800 large M&A transactions (over million euros) take place in the industrial sector in Germany each year. More than half of these investors are from outside Germany. In recent years, non-German shareholders have dominated DAX-listed blue-chip firms as industrial and financial players from all over the world have been keen to invest in Germany. Chinese companies are just following suit. The share of M&As related to the broader manufacturing industry will remain 60–80% in the future, but the composition will change. The proportion of the targets related to smart manufacturing, environmental protection, and new materials will rise. In addition, companies that tie in well with concepts such as Big Health and consumption upgrade will also be much sought after.

Authors What is your take on the restrictions China has imposed on outbound investments? What effect will these restrictions have on M&A activities in Germany?

Wang I think these measures are necessary. Massive capital outflows have a serious impact on developing countries and must be avoided. The risk of a potential bubble is limited, as almost all of the Chinese investments in Germany flow to industrial assets. However, last year did show signs of overheated outbound investment. Some investors didn't pay enough attention to the underlying quality of their target assets or the latent risks associated with them. As a result, the valuations of these companies were often inflated. Some investors were driven by short-term, speculative objectives and didn't care about synergy realization at all. However, this attitude has subsided following the implementation of the new rules. The Chinese firms that still go overseas for M&As are usually strategic investors with industrial operations and well-devised long-term plans. The financial investors are also generally those institutions with international investment experience and industry integration capabilities.

Although the total number of projects and transactions will remain higher than it was from 2010 to 2015, overall numbers will drop from the peak seen in the growth-spurt year of 2016. Annually, we can expect to see just over 20 acquisitions from China, including 4–8 acquisitions worth over 100 million euros, and possibly a small number of acquisitions worth over a billion euros.

Authors What do you think about the tighter controls on M&As that have been put in place by Germany and other Europe countries? Will this become a lasting trend?

Wang Germany is a relatively open economy. The new government regulations haven't triggered any fundamental changes, as the new regulations primarily focus on safeguarding key infrastructure, which is not the main target of Chinese investment. Previously, if the German Ministry for Economic Affairs didn't initiate a review of a non-declared transaction within 3 months, it was automatically deemed that the government didn't have any objections. Now, the ministry has 5 years to launch a review. For this reason, it is highly recommended to apply for approval from the German government. However, even before the new regulations, most of the companies in deals we handled did this anyway. In short, I believe the impact of the new regulations will be insignificant.

Authors China's position in Germany is now being contested by investors from other developing countries, especially the other BRICS nations. Compared to investors from other countries, what advantages do Chinese investors have?

Wang India is the only developing country that can compete with China in terms of the number and size of M&A deals, but India lacks an advanced manufacturing industry. While it has a few outstanding large-scale conglomerates, India is far behind in terms of the sheer number of competent medium-sized enterprises in China. Furthermore, the financing environment for medium-sized enterprises is often worse than for Chinese companies and a stable, unified market is something their Indian counterparts lack. These factors explain why prominent Indian investments are quite rare in Germany despite several cases of major European companies being acquired by Indian conglomerates. As India's level of industrialization is about a generation behind China, many of the target companies acquired by Indian firms are positioned at the low-end of the market with relatively low technical know-how and poor future development prospects.

Authors Recently, equity investment has been the main form of investment for Chinese companies in Germany. Will other forms of investment, such as bond, asset, and greenfield investments become more prominent in the future?

Wang There is expected to be an increase in bond investments and acquisitions of significant minority interests in listed companies (20% is roughly the required threshold to exert influence on the target firm). For example, in 2016, PwC Germany helped Chiho-Tiande use bond investments to take over Scholz Group, Germany's largest company in the metal recycling sector with sales of more 3 billion euros. This was also the largest business bond restructuring and acquisition case in Germany last year. However, it is hard for asset and greenfield investments to achieve significant growth.

Authors We presented three successful cases in this book, but we also know about numerous failures. Based on your experience, what are the main differences between the Chinese buyers in successful and unsuccessful M&A cases?

Wang The success or failure of an M&A is often determined before the transaction. I believe the key to a successful M&A is not to choose a cheap target, but to choose the right target. If an M&A is unsuccessful it is not because the target was expensive, but because it was simply wrong. Correct strategic decisions and professional transaction processes account for around 80% of the success. The target is right when it fits with the acquirer's own growth strategy and its individual characteristics. Genuine core competitiveness can be translated into synergy.

Authors Most of the Chinese companies that we have been exposed to have chosen to retain the management teams of the companies they acquire and only a few members of staff are sent from China to take on roles in finance or management control. How do you explain this decision? Will this change in the future?

Wang For lack of experience in overseas M&As, Chinese firms attach great importance to ensuring a smooth transition during the post-M&A phase. Sometimes the importance they attach is excessive. For example, some of the target companies may need to use the arrival of a new owner as an opportunity to change their public image or make adjustments to their strategic course, work processes, company culture, or personnel. We can see that Chinese enterprises are becoming more and more experienced and confident. The initial retention of the incumbent management does not mean that the status quo will be maintained indefinitely. As the German subsidiary integrates into the Chinese holding firm over time, the number of structural adjustments and staffing changes will increase.

In the past, we have seen that Chinese investors tend to value the loyalty of the German management more than their professional competence or fit within the company. An increasing number of Chinese firms give the national managers of their acquired German firms executive positions within the parent company. Although this ensures a certain degree of loyalty, the investors often overlook the fact that regional managers may lack global strategic vision and managerial aptitude.

Authors When asked about their motivation for acquiring German companies, Chinese companies usually cite a combination of German advanced technological competence with the huge potential of the Chinese market. In our view, however, only very few firms are able to achieve this, particularly in the consumer goods industry. What do you think is the biggest obstacle?

Wang The success rate has a lot to do with the competence and the absorptive capacity of the Chinese firms. The more systematized and integrated the product is, the harder it is to absorb. In contrast, the more standardized and modularized the product is, the easier it is to absorb. In addition, if synergy mainly lies in the sales network, it is important to determine whether the Chinese firm and its German subsidiary share the same target customer groups.

Success is much more uncertain in consumer goods than in industrial goods. The quick implementation of synergies in the consumer goods sector is impeded by having such a large the customer base, highly changeable requirements, higher distribution costs, and requiring higher investment in brand building, etc. For this reason, suitable M&A targets should be found in niche markets with few international competitors, resilient domestic demand, a stable customer base, sufficient space for imported substitutes, and an existing marketing and sales network.

Authors How do you view the role works councils play prior to an acquisition and during the integration phase? What is your take on the cooperation between the works council and Chinese investors?

Wang The role of the works council in the transaction process is minor. At small and medium-sized private firms, or even listed companies, the works councils have almost no impact. Only in large traditional industrial conglomerates does the works council have real power. When they sell non-core businesses, the group works council (konzernbetriebsrat) and the employee organization of the target company will often express dissent. Although they cannot prevent the deal, management will generally consider the concerns of the works council and require the acquirer to keep as many jobs as possible in Germany or the acquirer may promise not keep the factory open and retain all members of staff for a certain number of years.

After the acquisition, works councils and employee committees can be good collaboration partners. In light of the pressures of globalization and the tendency of employees and employers in the German-speaking countries try to reach a compromise, the involvement of the works council is usually constructive. While cooperation and building mutual trust are important, Chinese firms also need to be able to confront the works council when necessary in order to achieve the best outcomes.

Authors The transfer of know-how is a sensitive topic, but in the long run, this is the central goal of Chinese investors, as this is the only way for Chinese companies to grow their revenue generation capacity. In your experience, what approach do companies with good track records tend to follow in this matter?

Wang Project-based cooperation and training help the parent company increase its technical capabilities. In turn, this generates a boost for the development of the German subsidiary.

Authors What are the key challenges when integrating a newly acquired company?

Wang Integration is about dealing with the specific situation in the most appropriate way and finding the right solution for the "bugs" that emerge. Acquired companies with poor performances are likely to require adjustments in virtually all area, such as strategy, organizational structure, processes, product mix, R&D, design proposals, personnel, and financial management. Setting the right pace and priorities is crucial. After all, the key challenges may change in importance at different times.

Authors What are the differences and similarities in terms of the M&A strategy and the post-investment management of state-owned and private enterprises? How do you evaluate their respective strengths and weaknesses?

Wang In fact, we do not think that there is any substantial difference between state-owned and private enterprises. Some SOEs may be more concerned about their market position, the ranking of the company, and fit with national strategies. Private enterprises may be more concerned about the long-term return on investment and capital market performance. In the process of integration, the staffing arrangements of SOEs are less flexible than those of private enterprises. If integration runs into difficulties, SOEs are more likely to cease implementing the necessary adjustments due to concerns about their corporate image. The content of SOEs' internal books, such as financial booking, can be more complicated than for private enterprises. In terms of management models after acquisitions there is no significant difference because business management is the essentially the same at both types of company.

An important issue for SOEs is that the management system and practices of German companies may change if the CEO is removed from their position as chairman or general manager. In this regard, private enterprises have more stability than the SOEs.

Authors Thank you for your value insights and we wish PwC Germany further success.

10 Interview with Mr. Zhang Huanping, General Manager of Eurasian Consulting

This interview was conducted on July 26th 2017 and was published with kind permission of Mr. Zhang Huanping.

Zhang Huanping is founder of Eurasian Consulting and a renowned expert in Sino-German M&A.

10.1 About Eurasian Consulting

Eurasian Consulting was founded in Frankfurt am Main, Germany in 2004 by Zhang Huanping. In the early days, Eurasian Consulting's main business focus was to provide German companies with consulting services on topics, such as investing in China, securing financing, and developing joint venture cooperation. Since 2007, Eurasian Consulting has reoriented its core business, strengthening its consulting activities in the area of strategic implementation for M&As between European and Chinese corporations. The firm has successfully accomplished several cross-border M&A cases, which have had enormous influence on their respective industries. For this reason, Eurasian Consulting has become a leader in the field of M&A consulting between China and Europe.

Authors What are the factors that drive Chinese companies to go overseas for mergers and acquisitions (M&As)? Have these factors changed since a decade ago?

Zhang We believe there are three main driving factors: brands, technology, and global business platform. These all take time to build, and time is something that most Chinese companies don't have. So overseas M&As are the only way for Chinese companies to achieve these strategic goals in a short space of time. These factors don't seem to have changed since 2007, but as Chinese companies grow more experienced in overseas M&As, they are becoming more selective and the demands they set on target companies

J. Y. Yang et al., *Chinese M&As in Germany*, Management for Professionals,
https://doi.org/10.1007/978-3-319-99405-5_10

higher than they were. As well as focusing on the three main points, greater attention is being given to the capacity of the target firm to generate future cash flows. As the size of these transactions grows, core financial indicators increasingly cannot be ignored in M&A decisions.

Authors Why is Germany so attractive to Chinese companies? What will be the trending industries for investment in Germany in the next few years?

Zhang According to the Country-risk Rating of Overseas Investment from China (2016), out of more than 190 Chinese overseas investment destinations, Germany has the best investment environment and Germany is also Europe's largest economic entity with a high proportion of hidden champions in the various market segments. For a variety of historical reasons, most of them are small and medium-sized enterprises or family businesses. Due to high production costs in Germany, it is necessary for companies to constantly improve their technology and enhance competitiveness of their brand to ensure their long-term survival. This is exactly the kind of acquisition target Chinese companies are looking for. Further, unlike the highly competitive relationship between China and the United States, the relationship between China and European countries is often based more on cooperation than competition. Overseas M&A activities in Germany or elsewhere in Europe can achieve a greater synergistic effect.

According to current market demand, we believe that industrial automation, health care, and electric vehicles will be the primary sectors for M&As over the next few years. Although Germany is not a forerunner in the area of electric vehicles, we believe that Germany has sufficient technical capital to catch up and overtake the current leaders, after all, many of the world's top automotive OEMs and suppliers are situated here in Germany.

Authors We presented three successful cases in our book, but we also know about numerous failures. Based on your experience, what are the main differences between the Chinese buyers in successful and unsuccessful M&A cases?

Zhang Since Eurasian Consulting was founded in 2004, we have successfully completed dozens of Sino-EU M&A cases. Looking at these companies today, it seems that the cases we have dealt with have all produced positive outcomes. While it is undeniable that advantageous market circumstances contributed to the some of these successes, we believe that the overriding factor of a successful M&A project is that the Chinese acquiring company must have a very strong desire to have overseas subsidiaries and be extremely clear on its strategic objectives. Furthermore, the investors that have been successful have considerable financial capacity and are highly capable at implementing changes in China. Finally, it is necessary for them to have the ability to steer the target enterprise strategically, and to onboard and motivate the local management. All in all, successful mergers and acquisitions are those that are able to unleash the synergy between the acquirer and the target to the fullest extent.

Authors Most of the Chinese companies that we have looked at have chosen to retain the management teams of the companies they acquire, while only a small number of staff are sent from China, usually to take on financial or management control roles. How do you explain this phenomenon? Will this change in the future?

Zhang Compared to Western countries, China is clearly lagging behind in terms of the maturity of its market economy and internationalization. As a result, most Chinese companies are unable to run a global enterprise as they are not familiar with overseas markets and lack the ability to manage at a micro level. Therefore, one of the most important considerations in overseas M&As is whether the target company's incumbent management can remain in place once the deal is closed. Fortunately, most Chinese companies are aware of their deficiencies in this area, which is why they tend to only send a few hand-picked managers to help develop the new entity following the acquisition. It is not hard to find examples of overseas M&A cases that failed due to the excessive involvement of the investor's management team in the daily operations of the acquired company. Even companies with plenty of experience in international operations from established markets, such as the US and Japan have fallen into this trap. Most M&As by Chinese companies benefit the parties involved, as the inventors are willing to see themselves as a humble learners and don't assume it is necessary to send a management team to lecture on how to run day-to-day business. We don't think this phenomenon will change. First of all, China does not have sufficient numbers of talented managers with adequate international experience. Nurturing talent is a slow process. Second, even with such a talent pool, it is still not advisable to parachute in a Chinese team to manage foreign companies, not to mention running the post-merger integration phase.

Authors When Chinese companies are asked about their motivation for acquiring German companies, they often cite a desire to combine Germany's advanced technology with China's huge market potential. In our view, only a very few firms can accomplish this goal and there have been several notable failures, especially in the consumer goods sector. What do you think is the biggest obstacle to making this combination a success?

Zhang Whether in consumer goods or industrial sectors, German companies' R&D efforts are primarily technology-driven and focus more on the high-end market. In contrast, the market for high-end industrial products in China is not particularly large, so the assumption that combing high-end technology with the huge potential of the Chinese market will guarantee success is false. For Chinese companies, the real advantage of acquiring a German company with a technology-rich brand is to obtain the technical know-how that will enable the investor to develop products specifically for the Chinese market. By moving away from technology-oriented development to market-oriented development, market penetration can be maximized. While gradually transforming high-end products to mid-end products, their quality and cost performance will also improve, making them more competitive and tailoring them to the demands of the vast Chinese market.

Authors The transfer of technical know-how is a sensitive topic. However, this is the core long-term goal of Chinese investors, as it is the only way for Chinese companies to ensure future revenue growth. In your experience, what approach do successful companies tend to choose?

Zhang We believe the aim of M&As should not be to acquire technology, as the benefit this provides is transient. Instead, companies should aim to acquire a research and development platform, which will have a long-lasting effect. The advantages generated by existing product designs and manufacturing processes are always short-lived. Combining the R&D platform of foreign enterprises with the knowledge of a local R&D team is a reliable way to improve the parent company's revenue generation capabilities.

Authors What are the key challenges in integrating a newly acquired entity? How do these challenges change with time as integration progresses?

Zhang The integration phase is a key step in the success of an M&A project and it is necessary for this to take place gradually. The often-mentioned 100- and 365-day periods after the M&A mark the important timeframes for short-term integration. After M&As, the management and the customers of the merged company will anticipate some changes to the company. To ensure a smooth transition, the new shareholders should seize this opportunity to implement some integration plans, such as governance systems, financial booking, corporate financing, and sharing purchasing and marketing channels, etc. However, in the long run, the biggest challenge for post-merger integration is how to achieve synergies and how to ensure the Chinese and German teams can work well with each other, complementing the advantages the other brings to the table.

Authors What are the differences and similarities between the M&A strategies and the post-investment management approaches of state-owned and private enterprises? What are their respective strengths and weaknesses?

Zhang Overseas M&As are often a result of long-term strategic considerations. At private enterprises, the company's owners are usually the key decision-makers, so to be able to proceed in this direction, it is vital that they are convinced of the advantages that M&As offer and that they have the determination to see them through to the end. However, if the decision-makers at private companies are fully onboard with the M&A, these companies tend to outpace state-owned enterprise in the progress they make. Private enterprises also have more advantages in the post-merger integration phase by being able to offer incentive plans for the management team. In addition, the M&A teams of private enterprise are more professional, have stronger market acumen, and their negotiating strategies are more in line with international norms. On the other hand, the advantages of state-owned enterprises mainly lie in their market power and risk resilience. Furthermore, the leading position in certain areas accelerates entry into the Chinese market for firms acquired by state-owned enterprises more than those acquired by private enterprises. Overall, we believe that private and listed enterprises are playing an increasingly important role in overseas M&As and are gradually outperforming state-owned enterprises.

Authors Thank you for your value insights and we wish Eurasian Consulting a bright future.

Reference[1]

Invest in China. (2016). Foreign direct investment statistics.

[1]Apart from those indicated in the figures, the authors consulted some other sources as follows. It cannot be excluded that some references found on internet may not be included here for lack of explicit source.

Part IV

Challenge Accepted

To help the reader contextualize the recent cross-border M&A activities by Chinese firms, we will briefly review the history of foreign direct investment (FDI) worldwide before discussing the trends shaping Chinese M&As in Germany over the last few years.

The FDI landscape changed dramatically in Germany in 2016, as direct investment from China outstripped investment in the other direction for the first time. It is hardly surprising that Chinese investors are attracting a lot of attention from the media, politicians, and business communities. Despite this prominence, the vision these Chinese firms and the growth paths following the acquisitions are complete remain largely unknown to the broader public. Unfortunately, only a small number of individuals outside of the companies involved are aware of this aspect of M&As from China.

We have had the privilege to write three in-depth case studies on this subject, in which we reflect on the first-hand insights we gained from speaking directly to the key stakeholders. In doing so, we hope to demystify the potential concerns about Chinese investors. As stated earlier, Chinese investors tend to have a longer investment horizon and, in many cases, do not plan to sell their acquired German entities any time in foreseeable future. As our research continues, we hope to enrich our findings over time, and offer these as a foundation for further study into Chinese M&A activities abroad.

In this chapter, we will highlight the key findings from the case studies and will conclude by sharing our thoughts about Chinese M&A activities in the coming years.

11 Key Findings of Post-M&A Integration by Chinese Investors in Germany

Previous chapter features three case studies with three Chinese acquiring companies: the SGSB Group, previously known as ShangGong, the CIMC Group, and Joyson Electronics. The first two are state-owned enterprises and the latter is a privately owned company. In what follows, we highlight the commonalities and differences between their approaches to post-M&A integration, which offers a lens through which to understand Chinese investors' value creation strategy.

11.1 Motive and Strategy

The three Chinese firms were looking for growth opportunities and viewed the acquired German firms as growth partners rather than cash cows. The senior managers of the Chinese acquirers are reluctant to refer to themselves as "investors", a term that is often associated with short-sightedness or self-centralism in China. Instead, they prefer to identify themselves as "integrators" or even "value creators". None of the Chinese acquirers presented in the cases plan to sell their German subsidiaries any time soon. The long-term investment horizon sets the Chinese apart from the rest of the investor crowd. Such mindset is commonplace among Chinese firms that have acquired firms overseas in recent years, implying that the Chinese do not rely on financial engineering, as is typical of PE funds with finite exit windows.

Although the integration process was at different stages at the three firms, a pattern was observable across the cases. The companies successfully set the basics right early on and soon started exploiting top-line potential. After all, no company becomes a world leader by cost cutting only.

Despite the common goal of pursuing of strategic assets, there are nuances to the motivations behind each of the acquisitions. SGSB was grappling with great uncertainty over its own fate when it started negotiations to acquire the sewing machine specialist Dürkopp Adler, which had also been struggling to make a profit for a long time. SGSB was in urgent need of reforming itself and looked to acquisition of a

J. Y. Yang et al., *Chinese M&As in Germany*, Management for Professionals,
https://doi.org/10.1007/978-3-319-99405-5_11

foreign company as one last resort. It had been a bumpy journey since the acquisition, but Dürkopp Adler made it, surviving the economic downturn in 2009 and keeping its technological edge, thanks to the unwavering support it received from its Chinese mother company. Now Dürkopp Adler is well-poised to strive for worldwide market leadership. A weak–weak situation was turned around to a win–win situation for both SGSB and Dürkopp Adler.

CIMC was actually one of the first Sino-foreign joint ventures in China to be co-founded and managed by foreigners, although it does have strong ties to the government. CIMC became interested in Ziegler, the bankrupt firefighting and rescue equipment manufacturer, because Ziegler's airport rescue-truck product was thought to complement CIMC's airport facilities portfolio. While this was indeed the case, it became clear fairly soon that the firefighting business could be a lucrative business with excellent growth prospects in its own right.

Joyson Electronics, the only privately owned company featured in the cases, is a very young company. Just 7 years after its foundation in 2004, it acquired Preh GmbH, a leading automotive supplier of electronic components, from the private equity house Deutsche Beteiligungs AG. Joyson Electronics was in urgent need of Preh's expertise regarding electronic parts as well as direct access to the leading OEMs to build its automotive electronics business and, more importantly, move up the value chain for better margins and sustainable growth.

In a nutshell, the motivations of the Chinese acquirers can be characterized along two dimensions: the urgency to acquire new entities; and their relevance to the company's existing core business. The Chinese firms featured here can be roughly plotted on the matrix below (see Fig. 11.1). The diagram presents a snapshot shortly before or at the moment of the acquisition. However, motive is not static and shifts over time, as seen in the case of CIMC, where Ziegler's relevance to its parent company's core business increased, when the potential the firefighting and rescue business for the group as a whole surfaced.

Coincidentally, none of the Chinese acquiring companies said they had a clearly defined strategy for value creation prior to the acquisitions. ShangGong Europe's first comprehensive growth strategy was officially introduced almost 12 years after the acquisition; CIMC originally wanted to integrate Ziegler into its airport facilities business; and while Joyson Electronics was clear about entering the electronic parts sector from the beginning, it did not have an official value creation strategy before the acquisition either. The Chinese acquirers followed their gut-feelings, focusing on the direction of the strategy instead of the details. They are also pragmatic and play by ear, honing their strategy skills as integration deepens. The good news for the acquired firms is that the Chinese acquirers treat them as equal partners, who co-evolve over time through mutual learning and leveraging.

Fig. 11.1 Motivation of Chinese acquirers. Source: compiled by authors on basis of case studies

11.2 Corporate Governance

The incumbent management teams, works councils, and staff of the acquired firms are prone to have concerns about incoming Chinese owners, mainly stemming from their limited experience with the far-off Asian country. Indeed, Chinese firms have a much shorter track record with M&A's than many of their Western counterparts and they lacked experience in dealing with the large number of stakeholders they encountered, when they first expanded overseas. It has been a learning process on both sides.

Being sensible about their shortcomings, Chinese acquirers tend to leave the target companies' management teams intact, as they are more familiar with the local market and stakeholders, such as customers, suppliers, employees, and lenders. The continuity of the business is in the interest of virtually every party involved.

The three acquired companies featured in these case studies have different legal forms. Dürkopp Adler, a publicly traded company, is an "Aktiengesellschaft" (stock corporation) by default. Both Preh and Ziegler are "Gesellschaften mit beschränkter Haftung" or "GmbH" for short (private limited companies).

The two-tier board system which emerged in the 1870s, consists of the "Vorstand" (management board) and the "Aufsichtsrat" (supervisory board). In stock corporations and large limited liability companies, the two tiers of board have to be separate. The management board consists only of internal directors and is charged with managing

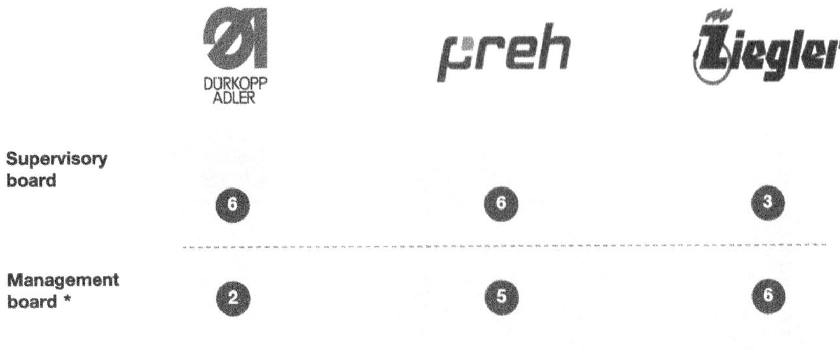

* "Vorstand" in the case of Dürkopp Adler, "Geschäftführung" for Preh and Ziegler

Fig. 11.2 Board structure of the German firms after acquisition. Source: compiled by authors on basis of case studies

the company. The supervisory board, comprising of at least three members, appoints and supervises the management board. For firms with over 500 employees, at least one third of the board members should be staff representatives. The members of the management board and the supervisory board must not overlap.

The size and constellation of the management teams vary widely, as demonstrated by the three cases we presented. Dürkopp Adler has a six-member supervisory board with two members on its management board. Preh's two boards have roughly equal numbers on each. Ziegler's board structure is the opposite of Dürkopp Adler as its management board is larger than its supervisory board (see Fig. 11.2).

Dürkopp Adler's supervisory board has three Chinese faces: Zhang Min, chairman of DA's supervisory board and CEO of parent company SGSB Group; Fang Haixiang, deputy chairman of DA's supervisory board and deputy CEO of SGSB Group; and Xiaolun Heijenga, a tax consultant based in Germany. The management board consists of Zheng Ying and Michael Kilian.

In the case of Preh, Joyson's founder and CEO, Jeff Wang, and vice president, Jimmy Guo, sat on the supervisory board after the acquisition of Preh. Jimmy left the board a couple years later, while Jeff stays. After the takeover, the incumbent chairman of the supervisory board, Scheffels retained his position. He is also a board member at DBAG, the previous owner of Preh. In 2016, Michael Roesnick resigned as spokesman of the management board and replaced Rolf Scheffels as chairman of the supervisory board, which Scheffels continues to serve on. On Preh's five-person management board, Charlie Cai is the only Chinese national sent by Joyson Electronics. He is responsible for supply chain management and the commercial vehicle business.

Ziegler is the unique case among the three, as both the supervisory board and the management board are headed by Chinese nationals. Li Yinhui, head of CIMC's airport facilities business unit, is chairman of the supervisory board, while Luan

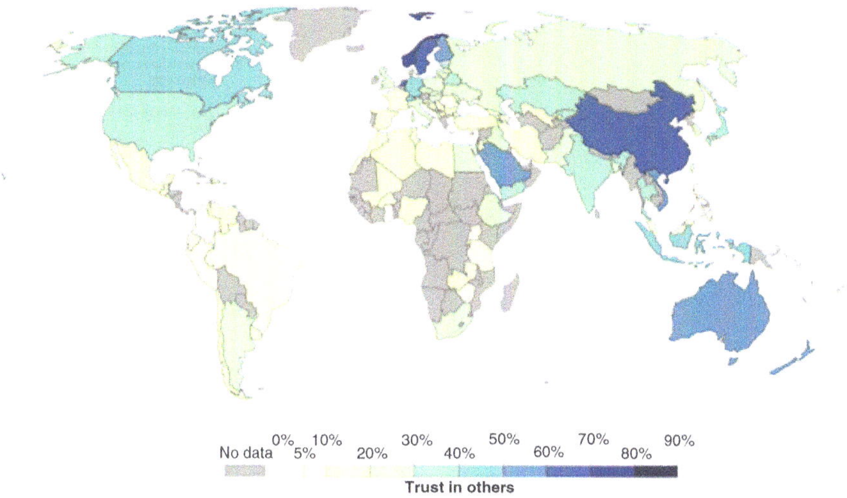

Fig. 11.3 Trust Index—World Value Survey (share of people who agree with the statement "most people can be trusted"). Source: Trust—World Value Survey

Youjun assumes overall responsibility for operations, supported by a diverse European management team.

In all three cases, the Chinese mother company refrained from parachuting managers to the German entities on the ground of not wanting to interfere with daily operations. Chinese managers know from their own experience that management should be driven by outcome, not by formality. At many Sino-foreign joint ventures founded after the introduction of the Reform and Opening-up Policy, it used to be common practice to appoint one Chinese manager and one foreign manager in each department within the company. In hindsight, the dual-management structure was not a good idea, as management efficacy and efficiency suffered from red tape and mistrust.

The Chinese acquirers learned from this lesson and granted the local management team considerable latitude to exercise managerial discretion. The total number of representatives from the Chinese investor is always limited, no matter what roles they play within the company. One could argue that the Chinese had no option but let the incumbent team run the business in the absence of skilled Chinese managers. An alternative but tempting theory is that the Chinese are simply more trusting, as a world value survey on trust attitudes of different nationalities shows (Fig. 11.3).

11.3 Integration and Transformation

With the light-touch approach, Chinese investors tread carefully when integrating and transforming their newly acquired companies. Meanwhile, the incumbent management team is charged with a central role in the integration process. All three cases

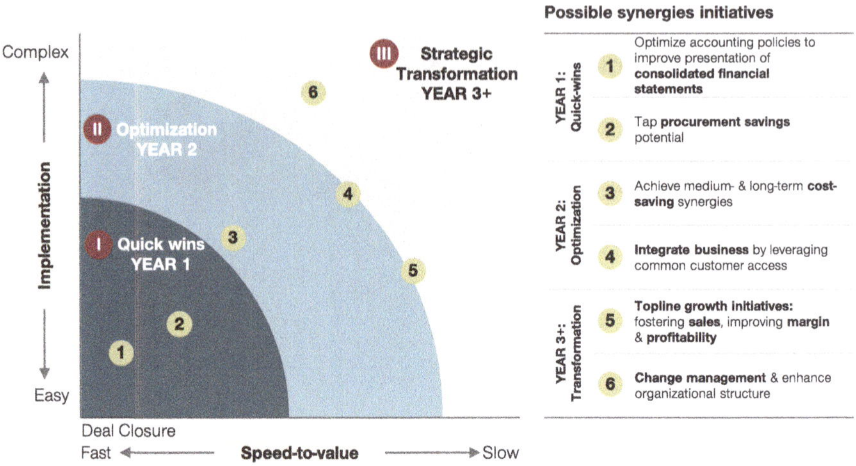

Fig. 11.4 Post-M&A integration roadmap. Source: Simon-Kucher and Partners, KPMG

have shown that the Chinese acquirers deliberately follow a laissez-faire strategy, which panned out well. SGSB and Joyson Electronics outperformed their industry peers by far in shareholder value creation; and CIMC succeeded in restoring the profitability of a bankrupt firm in just 3 years.

Post-M&A integration typically unfolds in three phases (see Fig. 11.4). Experience shows that top-line growth is particularly important to long-term value creation. Cost-cutting is essential but has limited upside potential. Generally speaking, strategic transformation usually starts in the third year after the acquisition, focusing on change management and top-line growth initiatives, typically through smart innovations. The timeline represents a rule of thumb. Some acquirers do manage to tap on top-line initiatives early on; others wish that they had tackled the revenue management issues earlier.

The Chinese acquirers featured in the case studies have more or less accomplished phase one, “quick-wins”, and phase two, “optimization”, and now are walking through phase three, “strategic transformation”. Together with their Chinese shareholders, the German firms are pursuing business opportunities by engaging new products and/or new customer segments. In the meantime, organizational optimization is underway to facilitate this transformation.

The M-Type series epitomizes Dürkopp Adler’s continuous efforts to innovate. If it were not for SGSB’s support, new product development could have ceased in the aftermath of the 2008 financial crisis. The commitment to innovation has allowed Dürkopp Adler to defend its technology leadership worldwide. In response to megatrends like Industry 4.0 and Internet of Things, Dürkopp Alder has developed a state-of-the-art network solution dubbed Qondac 4.0. It is the first solution of its kind in the sewing machine industry and won the prestigious Texprocess Innovation Award in 2017. The beauty of Qondac 4.0 lies in its compatibility, i.e. the application works on every brand of sewing machine with a connectivity function and is not restricted to captive brands. With help of Qondac 4.0, Dürkopp Adler is exploring unchartered territory and producing groundbreaking solutions for the industry.

In terms of its organization, Dürkopp Adler was, for a long time, synonymous with ShangGong Europe. ShangGong Europe was originally set up in 2004 as an investment vehicle for the SGSB Group in Europe and until 2013, Dürkopp Adler was the sole investment in its portfolio. With the acquisition of additional brands, such as Pfaff and KSL, ShangGong Europe took on greater and broader responsibilities, driving the SGSB Group's sewing machine business forward across the globe.

Preh's primary focus used to be the European markets, however, penetration into Chinese automotive OEMs accelerated considerably with Joyson Electronics becoming the new owner. At the time of the acquisition, the Chinese investor projected a double-digit annual growth rate for its business in China. The German managers were shocked and thought it was some kind of joke. Such a high growth rate was unheard of in Europe. However, the following years proved otherwise. The China business developed in line with the Chinese parent company's ambitious plan.

Battery Management Systems (BMS) used to be a subordinate business unit of Preh. Premium automotive brands, such as BMW and Daimler, turn to Preh for battery management solutions for their electric cars. In anticipation of surging demand for electric vehicles, Joyson Electronics' management persuaded Preh to separate out BMS as a strategic business unit and allocate more resources to further develop BMS for the Chinese market.

Joyson Electronics retained the incumbent German management team, which went on to play an instrumental role in the subsequent acquisitions of Innoventis, IMA, and Evena. It is hard to imagine that this would have been possible, had the acquiring company been a well-established firm from a developed economy.

Ziegler lost no time in embarking on top-line initiatives with the support of its parent company, CIMC. The Chinese group boasts a strong customer network, both domestically and overseas, providing Ziegler with access to prospective customers outside its core European markets. Among all, China presents a particularly remarkable growth opportunity, considering that Ziegler barely had any business there before. Cooperation with its sister firm Sichuan Chuanxiao is still at a fledgling stage, but looks promising. Thanks to CIMC's network, Ziegler has already closed several big deals with overseas customers and is set to win more contracts in the near future.

Top-line growth can take three different paths after a company is acquired (see Fig. 11.5). Starting from the status quo, the acquired firm can build on its existing product portfolio and reach out to new clientele (Path A). A case in point is Ziegler. Making use of CIMC's local network, it succeeded in selling existing products to customers in China, who had been difficult to reach.

Under Path B, growth is achieved by offering new products to existing customers. Acquisition costs for this are the lowest of all the paths, as entry barriers have already been overcome. Joyson Electronics had already been supplying functional parts to Shanghai Volkswagen. After acquiring Preh, it was able to extend its offering by adding higher-value electronic parts.

Path C is the most challenging one, as the firm moves completely out of its comfort zone, tackling new customers and new products at the same time. The latest innovation

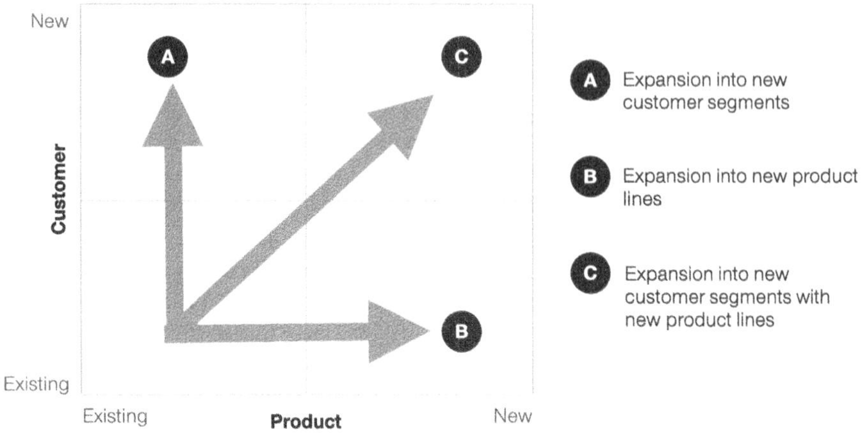

Fig. 11.5 Paths for top-line growth. Source: compiled by authors on basis of case studies

by Dürkopp Adler, Qondac 4.0, exemplifies such a path. At the time of writing, the new solution was being prepared for commercialization.

Concerning the roadblocks they encountered during the integration process, the managers involved in the three cases were unequivocal that culture and language barriers do exist but are by no means deal-breakers. As long as the visions are aligned, Chinese and Germans can work together just fine. Nevertheless, an open mindset is essential, as it is the prerequisite for mutual trust. Over time, both sides come to understand each other better. The Germans have realized that the Chinese are flexible because they believe in the mantra that the customers always come in the first place, whilst the Chinese have come to appreciate the Germans' rigor in business dealings. Some German business routines have consequentially found their way to the headquarters of the Chinese mother companies, such as budget review processes and meeting schedules, as seen in the case of Joyson Electronics/Preh.

That said, there are still differences that need to be reconciled. For example, speed to market varies significantly between Chinese and German firms. Chinese firms embrace the philosophy of "minimum viable product" and speed up new product development and production ramp-up, wherever possible. On the other hand, German companies traditionally are inclined to perform more checks and balances to be on the safe side, which may or may not lead to over-engineering. Furthermore, employees in Germany are entitled to more holidays and longer annual leaves and attach greater importance to private life. In China, employees are more ready to sacrifice personal life for work in exchange for the option of a sizable reward in future.

Often observed in recent acquisitions in Germany, the majority of Chinese acquirers have had reservations about integrating management teams. They are reluctant to second Chinese managers to the German subsidiaries. Our discussions with the Chinese manager community in Germany suggest that the management of the Chinese acquirers do not foresee this to change in the near future. In their view, the business should be run by the best possible people. Chinese managers overwhelmingly take on positions as some sort of coordinators, who do not directly participate in operations. Sanyi, a heavy-weight in construction equipment from China, even created a position of chief liaison officer based in Germany, after it acquired Putzmeister, a leading manufacturer of concrete pumps. Meanwhile, it is also rare for German managers to be transferred to the mother company in China.

In contrast, technological exchange is very much encouraged. Chinese and German engineers often work as a team on joint development projects, both in Germany and in China. In addition, at many firms, Chinese technicians regularly travel to Germany to attend different kinds of trainings. The German managers we interviewed shrugged off the accusation that Chinese investors are only after advanced technology when they conduct M&A's and that they are likely to walk away, as soon as they have assimilated the knowledge they were looking for. Their personal experience suggests that in today's dynamic world, technology turns obsolete sooner than anyone imagines. In addition to opening up additional revenue channels for the acquired firm, knowledge sharing helps loop in feedback from a broad clientele for improvement. In the end, the Germans are better off through sharing and co-developing new technology with their Chinese colleagues.

To the best of our knowledge, Chinese acquirers have, without exception, kept the brands of the German firms they have acquired. This is not particularly surprising as "Made in China" products are associated with low cost as well as low quality, whereas German brands signal high quality. With this being the case, Chinese acquirers often maintain two product lines, a premium line with the acquired German brand, and an economy line with their original Chinese brand.

But this situation may well change over time. Even the label "Made in Germany" was not born with glory—it was meant to have a negative connotation. The phrase traces its origins to when the UK passed the Merchandise Marks Act in 1887, which required the label to be placed on all German produce imported into the country. However, customers soon regarded it as a seal of quality and it acted as a free endorsement of German products.

11.4 Growth Initiatives

Only globalized firms will thrive in the future (Simon 2012). Based on his observations of firms based in Germany, Simon found that worldwide leaders in their niche markets, also known as hidden champions, always envision extremely ambitious goals, which stress overseas growth and market leadership, among others. Coincidently, Chinese acquirers in Germany also demonstrate such lofty ambitions, in that they stretch but not fit the growth trajectory of their German subsidiaries.

No matter what plan they have before the M&A, Chinese acquirers would set demanding growth objectives for their acquired German entities. As mentioned above, Joyson Electronics management aimed for double-digit growth for Preh's China business after the acquisition, which meant reaching the 1 billion yuan revenue mark within 5 years. This was an extremely bold target in German managers' view, but it was achieved. Ziegler laid out its 5-year strategy plan in 2016, which aimed for double-digit growth for 5 consecutive years, while the industry has low single digit growth. In 2016, ShangGong Europe, the backbone of which was Dürkopp Adler, crafted its first official growth strategy plan. In 5 years' time, it should overtake Juki as the world leader in industrial sewing machines. To put this into perspective, Juki's industrial machinery business unit is currently about three times the size of ShangGong's business in terms of revenue.

One shared feature of these ambitious plans is the commitment to top-line growth, be it through new products, new customer segments, or a combination of both. Growth potential is not confined to Germany and China. SGSB and Dürkopp Adler are penetrating Southeast Asia as a joint force, developing and marketing new products for the burgeoning region; Joyson Electronics and Preh serve customers together in all major markets; last not but least, Ziegler wins projects all over the world thanks to CIMC's extensive client network of airports.

Reference[1]

Simon, H. (2012). Hidden Champions - Aufbruch nach Globalia: Die Erfolgsstrategien unbekannter Weltmarktführer.

[1]Apart from those indicated in the figures, the authors consulted some other sources as follows. It cannot be excluded that some references found on internet may not be included here for lack of explicit source.

12 Closing Remarks on Chinese M&A Activities in Germany

Is China taking over Germany? Many German media have been saying so repetitively in recent time. But the reality is the opposite. China's share of total foreign direct investment stock in Germany accounts for less than one percent as of the end of 2016. More importantly, Chinese acquirers do play a different game than their western counterparts, in that they value and preserve the independence of the acquired firms to a large extent. This means that the German firms are not only contributing to the combined group by providing the Chinese mother companies with their know-hows, but also would gain access to strategic assets provided by the Chinese acquirers. These include financial support and market access to China as well as strategy, vision and even managerial know-hows, under circumstances.

Through M&A's in Germany, Chinese firms not only acquire strategy assets. But more importantly, they form partnership with the acquired firms and co-evolve towards market leadership in an accelerated fashion. Apparently, there is no single success recipe—every firm has to find its own growth path in the post-M&A phase. However, there exist some commonalities between recent cases. To begin with, the Chinese stand out from other investors due to their long-term perspective. They have the will and the patience to grow with their target firms. They prefer to keep management teams local, as they are more familiar with the market, customers, and other stakeholders, and they think big in terms of growth and market leadership. In line with their long-term focus, the last thing they want to do is to rush integration. Instead, they attach great importance to putting the right people in the right places. As Chinese managers generally lack the experience needed to take overall responsibility for a foreign entity, the Chinese acquirers send staff abroad to take roles usually in finance and management control. Recently, we have seen Chinese-owned firms in Germany hiring an increasing number of Chinese graduates from German universities, as the interaction with China grows in importance. Over time, the young talent educated in Germany will expect to contribute massively to the integration and transformation of German firms as well as their Chinese parent companies.

J. Y. Yang et al., *Chinese M&As in Germany*, Management for Professionals,
https://doi.org/10.1007/978-3-319-99405-5_12

Close cooperation between technical teams from China and Germany is already underway. They work together on joint product-development projects. Moreover, Chinese investors are more than willing to invest in German brands that they expect to achieve higher price premiums with in emerging markets, particularly China. Contrary to popular belief, the German firms acquired by Chinese acquirers do not really worry about their new parent companies stealing technology from Germany. Instead, sharing or co-developing new technology is seen as benefiting the group as a whole. Many instances support the tenet, where R&D and manufacture of high-end products have remained in Germany after acquisitions, while localization and mass production take place in China or other locations that offer a comparative advantage.

China's economy has evidently slowed down as it matures and rebalances itself toward consumption and services. While manufacturing will continue to play an important role for the foreseeable future, low-end/low-value-added manufacturing will gradually shift to neighboring countries in Southeast Asia. Nevertheless, China's growth rate remains among the highest globally. However, Chinese companies have turned to both domestic and outbound M&As to stem slowing growth in the home market. A wave of consolidations among small to medium-sized companies in China has reduced the number of domestic targets for Chinese buyers. Independent companies in China often prefer public market transactions or have high-value expectations, given local valuation benchmarks. This relative valuation gap is encouraging Chinese buyers to look abroad for targets.

The Chinese government has introduced a number of initiatives and policies to support strategic investment, both domestically and overseas. China's One Belt One Road initiative aims to enhance trade between Europe and Asia through a series of infrastructure investments in road, rail, and ports. The Made in China 2025 initiative seeks to move China's manufacturing sector upstream through technological upgrades and innovation. Consequently, a broad range of organizations are going abroad to look for M&A opportunities in their respective fields. SOEs, privates firms, and financial investors, including private equity funds and other investment firms, are now all participating in the wave of cross-border M&As. It has become such an overheated phenomenon that several governmental authorities have issued orders to tighten up controls on outbound investment in a similar way to how they deal with speculation.

We conclude the inaugural book with our eight predictions on the trends to watch out for regarding Chinese M&A activities in Germany over the next year:

1. Private and state-owned companies will both play an important role
2. Financial investors will become more active and compete for quality target firms, although they may not seek a controlling interest
3. Chinese investors will continue to be confronted with anti-globalization sentiment
4. German government may introduce tighter control on Chinese M&A activities in sensitive industries
5. Industry 4.0 and high-end consumer-goods-related businesses will remain hot targets for acquisitions

6. Chinese investor will rely heavily on the partnering approach for post-M&A integration in the foreseeable future
7. Joint innovation capabilities by both Chinese and German teams will become increasingly crucial to success as post-M&A integration unfolds
8. Chinese investors may resort to greenfield investment in Germany and Europe when attempted M&As fail.

References[1]

Baums, D. Corporate governance in Germany - system and current developments.
Deloitte. (2014). A new stage for overseas expansion of China's equipment manufacturing industry.
Destatis. (2016). Export by country.
EY. (2016). Chinesische Unternehmenskäufe in Europa - Eine Analyse von M&A-Deals 2005–2016.
Invest in China. (2016). Foreign direct investment statistics.
Liu, Y., & Woywode, M. (2013). Light-touch integration of Chinese cross-border M&A: The influences of culture and absorptive capacity. *Thunderbird International Business Review, 55*, 469–483.
Morgen, J. P. (2016). China's increasing outbound M&A.
Kale, P., Singh, H., & Raman, A. P. (2009). Don't integrate your acquisitions, partner with them. *Harvard Business Review, 87*(12), 87.
M&A Dialogue. M&A China - Deutschland, diverse editions from 2013 through 2016.
MERICS. (2016). Chinese investment in Europe. Mercator Institute for China Studies.
Mofcom. (2017). Chinese outbound foreign direct investment.
PwC.de. Various books on Sino-German cross-border transactions.
Simon, H. (2012). Hidden Champions - Aufbruch nach Globalia: Die Erfolgsstrategien unbekannter Weltmarktführer.
Thompson Reuter. (2016). Mergers and acquisitions review.

[1]Apart from those indicated in the figures, the authors consulted some other sources as follows. It cannot be excluded that some references found on internet may not be included here for lack of explicit source.

J. Y. Yang et al., *Chinese M&As in Germany*, Management for Professionals,
https://doi.org/10.1007/978-3-319-99405-5

The manufacturer's authorised representative in the EU is Springer Nature Customer Service Centre GmbH, Europaplatz 3, 69115 Heidelberg, Germany. If you have any concerns regarding our products, please contact ProductSafety@springernature.com

Printed and bound by CPI Group (UK) Ltd, Croydon, CR0 4YY
30/09/2026
02225261-0015